MW00962647

The **Best**
Craft Brewers,
Brewpubs
& Beer Bars in
the U.S. West

THE ULTIMATE BEER GUIDE: WESTERN EDITION

2017

Edited by Jamie Bogner, Trish Faubion, and Libby Murphy
Art direction and design by Jamie Bogner
Contributing writers: Jamie Bogner, Trish Faubion, Libby Murphy,
John Bolton, Dave Carpenter, Patrick Dawson, Jackie Dodd, Emily Hutto,
Steve Koenig, Heather Vandenengel, John M. Verive

Photography: Courtesy Melvin Brewing (13,15), Shawn "Flash" Parker (17),
Matthew Graves/mgravesphoto.com (19, 25, 33, 34, 39, 40, 51, 55, 71),
Jamie Bogner (21, 22, 24, 26, 27, 28, 29, 30, 31, 35, 37, 43, 57, 89, 91,
93, 96, 99, 100, 103, 105, 106, 108, 109, 121, 123), Marti Mills (45),
Courtesy Bittercreek Alehouse (53), Courtesy Emrich Office (59),
Hal Mooney (63), Jackie Dodd (75, 78, 82), Courtesy Brouwer's Café (77),
Taylor Abeel (110), Julie Verive (113, 115, 117), Lindsay Dawson (127)

Unfiltered Media Group, LLC
214 S. College Ave., Ste. 3
Fort Collins, CO 80524
beerandbrewing.com

ISBN: 978-0-9962689-9-8 (Print); 978-0-9977718-2-4 (eBook)
Library of Congress Control Number: 2016950834

Printed in China through Asia Pacific Offset

10 9 8 7 6 5 4 3 2 1

This book is dedicated to the adventurous beer fanatics who travel the country in search of great beer, and to the talented brewers who have applied themselves to the honorable duty of serving these fans. May your journey be fruitful and your glass always remain half full. Prost!

CONTENTS

MONTANA

Montana is a beautiful state with a vast expanse of wilderness and open sky. While the state has some local favorites that've been around for quite some time, it's a rapidly growing state when it comes to its craft-beer scene. For those expecting to settle into one place for a session, be aware of their liquor laws: only 48 ounces (three pints) can be served to one person in one day, and the beer taps shut down at 8:00 p.m.

BEST SPOTS FOR OLD SCHOOL BEER STYLES

Bayern Brewing's Bavarian-style beers and German-style restaurant are the height of old-school charm.

Carter's Brewing's saisons, weisses, and lagers make it a destination for German beer lovers.

BEST SPOTS FOR NEW SCHOOL BEER STYLES

Blackfoot River Brewing Company brews some USDA Organic beers.

Bozeman Brewing has a thriving experimental barrel program, as well as traditional beers.

BEST SPOTS TO ENJOY A MEAL WITH YOUR BEER

Montana Ale Works has a full array of upscale comfort foods and 40 taps of beer.

Great Northern Brewing in Whitefish has some incredible sandwiches and appetizers and GABF-winning beer.

MOST STYLISH TAPROOMS AND BARS

Draught Works' style is a mix of lodge chic and industrial pub.

Bayern Brewing makes you feel as if you've stepped into a Bavarian brew haus.

MOST AWARD-WINNING BREWERIES

1. Montana Brewing Co.
2. Red Lodge Ales
3. Great Northern Brewing Co.
4. Kettlehouse Brewing Co.

Montana Brewing Co. has earned an astounding 16 GABF medals and 11 World Beer Cup Medals.

BEST UNIQUE BEER EXPERIENCE

Big Sky Brewing has some award-winning brews and has three stages where national acts can entertain guests under the big, beautiful Montana sky.

Honorable mention: Draught Works has ski-in access.

BILLINGS

MONTANA BREWING CO.: When you make great beers, people notice—and judging by Montana Brewing's 16 Great American Beer Festival medals, people have definitely noticed. Quench your thirst with Whitetail Wheat, which has won 15 national medals, or Sandbaggers Gold, an English-style summer ale that's also got some hardware to brag about. A full-service kitchen serves up apps, sandwiches, burgers, and local specialties. The place is family-friendly, and you can take home a growler. **113 N. Broadway, Billings | montanabrewingcompany.com**

CARTER'S BREWING: The focus is all on the beer at Carter's, where you can order from 16 beers on tap while munching on popcorn in the tap room. Food can be ordered in, or bring your own. Kids are welcome, too—they serve root beer and juice and have a stack of games and cards to keep everyone entertained. Their Blackened CDA won the bronze at GABF, and over the past 5 years, they've taken home 18 medals at the North American Beer Awards. Take home a growler of one or two of your favorites! **2526 Montana Ave., Billings | cartersbrewing.com**

MISSOULA

BIG SKY BREWING COMPANY: Way up in the Montana Rockies lives Big Sky Brewing, which has been around for more than 20 years now. Because of Montana's liquor laws, the tap room can serve up to four 4-ounce samples of free beer. You can take home a growler, but don't plan on ordering a few pints and chilling for the afternoon. Their Moose Drool Brown Ale is perhaps their most well-known brew, and their Power Wagon Wheat Wine took home a World Beer Cup silver medal. They have a good lineup of IPAs, a wheat ale, and a Mexican lager, in addition to seasonal rotations. If you're visiting in the summer, you can catch a legit national act in their summer concert series, which happens in the field behind the brewery. Great views, great beer—who's going to say no to that? **5417 Trumpeter Wy., Missoula | bigskybrew.com**

BAYERN BREWING: When a trip to Munich is out of the question, take a trip to Bayern Brewing. Specializing in Bavarian-style beers, they have a tap list with 6 year-round beers and 9 seasonals. Their Dragon's Breath Dark Hef took home medals at the North American Beer Awards and the U.S. Open (twice!). While you're at the tap room, you can order from the upstairs Edelweiss Bistro, which serves traditional German foods, some of which include the brewery's beers in the recipe. Crowlers, growlers, and kegs are available to take home. **1507 Montana St., Missoula | bayernbrewing.com**

DRAUGHT WORKS: After a long day of mountain fun, ski in (you read that right) with friends and family to Draught Works for a pint to warm up. Fifteen beers round out the on-tap selection, and after you've settled on one, grab a friend and play some darts in the homey tap room. Notable beers include the Clothing Optional Pale Ale, "That's What She Said" Cream Ale, and Shadow Caster Red Ale. Their Scepter Head American Strong Pale Ale took home a gold at the GABF in 2014, and the GABF also crowned them Best Very Small Brewing Company of the Year. Live music is frequent, and they have a list of recommended delivery joints from which to get some grub. Although it'll be tricky, you can have your growler or keg filled before you ski it back to the car. **915 Toole Ave., Missoula | draughtworksbrewery.com**

KETTLEHOUSE MYRTLE ST. AND KETTLEHOUSE NORTHSIDE: Kettlehouse is actually two locations, both of which operate as a brewery and a tap room. Their Lake Missoula Amber took the bronze at North American Beer Awards, and their Olde Bongwater Hemp Porter won gold and bronze at NABA over two years. Eight beers are on draft in the tap rooms, and you can take home a crowler, growler, or even cans to go (at the Northside location only). Tours are available only through their KettleHouse Beer Kollege program, which is a free beer education program that teaches students the art of brewing and tasting craft beer.
North location: 313 N. 1st St. W., Missoula
South location: 602 Myrtle St., Missoula | kettlehouse.com

BIG SKY

LONE PEAK BREWERY: End a day at the largest ski resort in the United States with a locally made craft beer from Lone Peak. They offer up to 8 regular beers on tap and have a rotating list of seasonals and barrel-aged brews. Join the Pints Pass membership program during ski season for discounts on pints and growler fills. After a long day of skiing you'll want to order from their full food menu, which has something for just about everybody. **48 Market Pl., Big Sky | lonepeakbrewery.com**
BEEHIVE BASIN BREWERY: Take in some gorgeous mountain views from the tasting room at Beehive while sipping on one of their 10 rotating beers on tap. Their diverse beer lineup features a nice array of beers: porter, IPA, Belgian strong, cream ale, and more, with a barrel-aging program in the works. There isn't a kitchen on site, but you can bring your own or order in, and you can get your growler filled before you head out for more skiing. **245 Towncenter Ave., Big Sky | beehivebasinbrewery.com**

WHITEFISH

GREAT NORTHERN BREWING COMPANY: Whitefish is a destination in itself, so you'll want to add the state-of-the-art facility at Great Northern and a fresh pint to your outdoor adventure. Try their Wheatfish wheat lager, winner of the GABF 2013 silver and 2014 bronze in the Wheat Beer with Yeast category, or one of their annual Weathervane Seasonals. Take a tour of the brewery and go home with a growler, bottle, or keg full of your favorite brew. The draught house features a full food menu with sandwiches, salads, and apps, as well as live music and other events.
2 Central Ave., #1, Whitefish | greatnorthernbrewing.com

RED LODGE

RED LODGE ALES & SAM'S TAP ROOM & KITCHEN: After a day of exploring Yellowstone, hiking, or skiing, head over here to have a bite to eat, relax, and refuel with one of 7 year-round beers on tap or a rotating seasonal. The Bent Nail IPA is an intensely hopped brew that took home a bronze at GABF, and the Jacks 90 Scottish Ale is a rich amber ale that nabbed a silver at the North American Beer Awards—in fact, several of their beers have medaled at the North American Beer Awards. Kitchen fare is full service, with sandwiches, salads, apps, and a kids menu. Take a break on their back patio to enjoy the incredible Montana views or play some pool or darts inside. Growler fills are available. **1445 N. Broadway Ave., Red Lodge | redlodgeales.com**

BOZEMAN

BOZEMAN BREWING: Step inside this cozy tasting room, where you can settle down with 12 beers on tap. Six of those are brewed year-round, and include an IPA, pale ale, amber ale, hefe, and porter. Their seasonals run the gamut and include a barrel-aged selection here and there, too. Their North American Beer Award-winning Funky Virtue was aged in French Oak Port or Cabernet wine barrels, with additions of Oregon tart cherries and *Brett.* Food trucks are on site 5 nights a week, and you can head home with a growler or keg full of your favorite brew. **504 N. Broadway Ave., Bozeman | bozemanbrewing.com**

MONTANA ALE WORKS: This is the place to go when you're looking for a vast selection of regionally curated beers on tap. Forty taps strong, they serve up ales, IPAs, lagers, dark ales, wheats, and even some gluten-free selections. If you can't find what you're looking for on tap, ask about their bottle offerings. Cocktails and wine are also available, and the food menu features upscale comfort food including small plates, salads, burgers, and Montana-bred beef and bison. The space is massive, with 5 distinct areas to fit just about any type of experience you're looking for. **611 E. Main St., Bozeman | montanaaleworks.com**

HELENA

BLACKFOOT RIVER BREWING COMPANY: The brewers at Blackfoot are committed to creating true artisan ales, paying special attention to every ingredient in every beer they produce. Seven year-round beers can be found on draft at the brewery, including two USDA Organic beers, as well as a stout, Scottish ale, extra special bitter, IPA, and a cream ale. In addition to the year-round beers, they have a rotating seasonal program, as well as a weekly cask-conditioned firkin release. Stick around for live music or bring your growlers and fill up to go! **66 S. Park Ave., Helena | blackfootriverbrewing.com**

WYOMING

This Rocky Mountain state is packed with natural beauty—Yellowstone and Grand Teton National Parks being the crown jewels—but a small cadre of extremely talented craft brewers have put Wyoming beer on the national map. Whether you're in Jackson visiting the parks, Sheridan on the northern central border with Montana, or down in Laramie, there are award winning beers to be had.

BEST SPOTS FOR OLD SCHOOL BEER STYLES

Altitude Chophouse in Laramie excels at brewing tried and true examples of classic styles and pairs them with well-made classic and traditional pub fare.

BEST SPOTS FOR NEW SCHOOL BEER STYLES

Melvin Brewing in Alpine, Wyoming, has won the hops-centric Alpha King Challenge twice, and beers like 2x4 DIPA, Hubert Pale Ale, Brosaic DIPA, and others really push the limits of what's possible with hops.

BEST SPOTS TO ENJOY A MEAL WITH YOUR BEER

While Black Tooth Brewing doesn't have their own kitchen, the culinary approach to the beers from chef-turned-brewer Travis Zeilstra makes them perfect for pairing with the rotating food trucks.

MOST STYLISH TAPROOMS AND BARS

Snake River deserves credit for pioneering the industrial chic brewery look twenty years before it became the standard for every new brewery around.

MOST AWARD-WINNING BREWERIES

Snake River Brewing has far and away the most accolades of any Wyoming brewery, but Melvin/Thai Me Up and Black Tooth Brewing have come on strong in the medal count over the past few years.

BEST UNIQUE BEER EXPERIENCE

Thai Me Up's hyper focus on kung fu borders on psychosis, but this pint-sized powerhouse of a brew-pub is not to be missed.

MELVIN
BREWING

IPA

JACKSON

THAI ME UP: Melvin Brewing's Thai Me Up brewpub has two TVs—both play Kung Fu—but arguably, Thai Me Up, awarded the 2015 GABF Small Brewpub of the Year, is responsible for Jackson's best beer list. It has 20 taps, 10 dedicated to Melvin Brewing beers and 10 for the best beers that can be found in that part of the country. Since Melvin Brewing opened a new production facility in Alpine, the brewhouse at Thai Me Up is used to keep the beer list rotating with one-offs and experimental batches. Included in this lineup are copious double IPAs that come out of Melvin's RIIPA, the Rotational Imperial India Pale Ale series. Their food menu includes Thai-inspired eats and a burger for the less adventurous. **75 E. Pearl Ave., Jackson | thaijh.com**

SNAKE RIVER BREWING CO.: After a day of shopping and sightseeing in the super swanky Jackson, make your way over to Snake River Brewing, holder of 30 GABF and 16 World Beer Cup medals. Try the award-winning Pako's IPA, which some say is smooth-drinking and has a distinct citrusy, dank flavor. For something darker, the Zonker Stout is a foreign-style stout that's rich, roasty, and a touch chocolaty. After you've settled on something to drink, take a tour, order from their American fare food menu, or settle in for some family-friendly games. And don't forget to grab a growler or crowler to go! **265 S. Millward, Jackson | snakeriverbrewing.com**

WILSON

ROADHOUSE BREWING CO.: Refuel from a cold powder day at this award-winning brewery with experimental brews such as Tower of the Castle Sweet Potato Porter and Beautiful Buzz Espresso Stout. Beers on tap are constantly rotating, so you never know what you'll find on draft—better be sure to take some home in a growler just in case. The food menu carries upscale twists on old favorites and stick-to-your-ribs comfort food. **2550 Moose Wilson Rd., Wilson | roadhousebrewery.com**

ALPINE

MELVIN BREWING: Melvin's award-winning new 20,000-square foot production and packaging facility is located on 6 acres in Alpine, Wyoming, about 35 miles from Jackson (pictured above right). Although Melvin focuses on a hoppy beer list that sports five IPAs (Melvin IPA took home a bronze at GABF), they also make Belgians, imperial porters, coffee porters, and Jungle Juice, a red raspberry ale, and Heyzeus! (a Mexican lager). Chchchch-Cherry Bomb took gold at GABF for best American-Style Fruit Beer. The brewery is also developing a sour-beer program and soon will debut the Manual Release Series, an experimental series that focuses on barrel aging as well as different grains and yeast strains. You can taste many of Melvin's brews in the open, friendly brewery tap room that gives you a good view of the brewing operation, and the brewery plans to host tours and events. **624 Cty. Rd. 101, Alpine | melvinbrewing.com**

CASPER

KEG & CORK: This is the place to go for live bands—country (we are in Wyoming, after all) and Irish alike. But let's face it; we're not here just for the music. Twenty-eight taps make up the beer offerings at Keg & Cork, and if that's not enough you can choose from a healthy selection of whiskey and wines, too. Growler fills are available if you'd rather enjoy your beer in the comfort of your own home. Traditional Irish fare makes up a big part of the food menu, but American classics are also available. **531 Blackmore Rd., Casper | facebook.com/thekegandcork**

GALLOWAY'S PUB: Keg & Cork's sister pub has a little of the Keg & Cork vibe and more. Eighteen beers are on tap, but you can also grab some specialty shots and cocktails. The outside patio is a great place to unwind—even in the winter—with its fire pits and heaters, but summer visitors can play volleyball on their sand court. For the gamers, there's an on-site bowling alley, shuffle board, and beer pong. This is a 21+ establishment, so leave the kiddos at home. **2800 CY Ave., Casper | facebook.com/gallowayspub**

SHERIDAN

BLACK TOOTH BREWING: Founded by Travis Zeilstra (pictured at right), a chef, Black Tooth caters to customers who expect well-brewed classics more than cutting-edge combinations. The Wyoming market is more attracted to conservative styles of beer, and Black Tooth serves them up with an unparalleled eye for consistency. But while the beer styles might be traditional, look for exotic spice profiles—pink and Sichuan peppercorns, ginger, coriander, and yuzu juice, to name a few. Their approach has paid off, as evidenced by its multiple GABF, U.S. Open, and World Beer Cup trophies. Visit the brewery for a tour, 8 beers on tap, live music, and food trucks. **312 Broadway St., Sheridan I blacktoothbrewingcompany.com**

LUMINOUS BREWHOUSE: There's nothing better than a cold pint (or three) after a long day of exploring historic Sheridan, and with Luminous's 16 beers on tap, you'll have no shortage of ways to cool down— or warm up, depending on the season. Some of their most popular brews include the High Country IPA, Red Grade Ale, Java Moon Coffee Ale, and the X-X IPA. Hearty comfort food is available if you need to refuel with something other than beer. If you're looking to be entertained, stay a while to watch open-mic night, then go home with a growler. **201 Broadway St., Sheridan I luminousbrewhouse.com**

GILLETTE

GILLETTE BREWING COMPANY: Way up in northeast Wyoming, not far from Devil's Tower, in the sleepy town of Gillette, is Wyoming's first craft brewery. The nanobrewery offers 6 of their own brews on tap, as well as guest taps from other brewers. Their most popular brews include the Locomotive Brown, a chocolaty, nutty brew with vanilla, and Tall Canyon Porter, a smoky, rich dark beer. Come for a bite and order one of their signature hand-tossed pizzas, listen to some live music, and bring the kids—they're always welcome. Stay and watch some TV on one of their big screens or take a growler to go. **301 S. Gillette Ave., Gillette I gillettebrewingcompany.com**

LARAMIE

ALTITUDE CHOPHOUSE & BREWERY: Downtown Laramie has a gem of a brewery and chop house at Altitude, with a fist full of medals to show off. ALTbier took home gold at the World Beer Cup and North American Beer Awards, Pedal House Pilsner took home gold at NABA, as did Looking Glass Old English Ale and Lovesick IPA. Tumbleweat won bronze and silver at NABA and silver at GABF. And that's not to mention all the regional beer awards their beers have wrangled. The restaurant boasts some meaty dishes as well as burgers and pizza, and they have a kids' menu, too. They host frequent beer tastings and beer-and-food pairing events, but if beer is all you want, you can take home a growler of that, too. **320 S. 2nd St., Laramie I altitudechophouse.com**

LIBRARY SPORTS GRILLE & BREWERY: Eight house brews round out their offerings, with some interesting twists on old classics. Their Rattle-snake RyePA is an IPA with an aggressive hops profile and malty grains. For those seeking out a fruitier beer, they produce fruity wheats, IPAs, and shandies. The upstairs lounge is a cozy place to play pool, watch a game on the big screen, or—of course—read a book. Pizza and specialty burgers are their mainstays, but their kitchen is full-service, so there's a nice variety. Take a growler to go, or stick around to watch a live music act. **201 E. Custer St., Laramie | librarysportsgrille.com**

CHEYENNE

FREEDOM'S EDGE BREWING CO.: On your way up to the Black Hills, stop at Freedom's Edge for one of 8 beers on tap. Three IPAs, a pale ale, wheat ale, cream ale, and porter make up their beer list, and if you find one you love, take it in a growler to go. Food trucks are on site on a regular basis, but check the website for the schedule. Live bands visit here, and kids and dogs are welcome. **1509 Pioneer Ave., Cheyenne | freedomsedgebrewing.com**

COLORADO

Colorado is a craft-beer lover's state, with more than 300 breweries serving a population of around 6 million people, and options for every type of beer or experience under the 300 days of sun. From classic German-style lagers to mixed-fermentation sours, New England-style IPAs, and barrel-aged imperial stouts, Colorado breweries brew diverse styles and brew them well.

BEST SPOTS FOR OLD SCHOOL BEER STYLES

Zwei and Prost for classic German-style lagers, New Belgium for Belgian-style dubbels and tripels plus their wooden foeder-soured beers, Hogshead for traditional hand-pulled English-style cask ales.

BEST SPOTS FOR NEW SCHOOL BEER STYLES

Crooked Stave (right) for sour beers with as many different fruits as you can possibly imagine, Odell for progressively hopped IPAs and pale ales, Casey Brewing and Blending for mixed-fermentation beer with local fruit, Weldwerks and Odd 13 for hazy New England–style IPAs.

BEST SPOTS TO ENJOY A MEAL WITH YOUR BEER

The chef-driven gastropub fare at Euclid Hall is hard to beat, and their beer list is top notch; Freshcraft offers a dual focus on creative food and the best in craft beer; Bull & Bush is the perfect spot for more traditional pub fare with a throwback interior to die for.

MOST STYLISH TAPROOMS AND BARS

Avery Brewing's new tap room and restaurant deliver amazing food and beer in a gorgeous setting, First Draft in Denver offers pour-your-own beer in a cool industrial space, New Belgium's funky tap room is the artiest of the bunch, Odell's tap room and patio are legendary.

MOST AWARD-WINNING BREWERIES

You might not expect it, but Coors' The Sandlot is the winningest in Colorado. Dry Dock, New Belgium, Left Hand, Bull & Bush, and Coors itself have all racked up serious hardware from the most respected competitions in the modern era.

BEST UNIQUE BEER EXPERIENCE

Trve Brewing's heavy metal-inspired tap room deserves this note for its black walls, animal skulls, metal soundtrack, and general foreboding.

DENVER DOWNTOWN AND LODO

Some of the hottest craft-beer spots in Colorado can all be found within walking distance (or quick Uber distance, at least) in downtown and LoDo...

FALLING ROCK TAPHOUSE: (right) The venerable Falling Rock Taphouse is not only a must-visit while in Denver, it's a cultural touchstone—a shared experience that instantly bonds you to legions of craft-beer fanatics who have passed through the same doors, experienced the same surly bartenders, and marveled at the phenomenal tap exclusives Falling Rock gets as a result of cultivating three decades of friendships in the craft-beer world. If it's on tap, try the New Belgium Rock Star Blend, a special sour blended from the foeders of New Belgium just for Falling Rock and its LoDo neighbor, Star Bar. **1919 Blake St., Denver | fallingrocktaphouse.com**

STAR BAR: A hipster "dive," it offers a killer list of taps and bottles, a comfortable patio, skeeball and foosball, and karaoke a couple of nights a week. It can get loud and rowdy on busier nights, but you can usually find some quiet out back on the patio. **2137 Larimer St., Denver | starbardenver.com**

MR. B'S LIQUOR: They pull out all the stops for GABF with special bottle releases all week making it a necessary stop for rare-beer hunters. Look for special brewery collaborations such as B Side Avarice (a collab with River North) or Battonage (with Crooked Stave). **2101 Market St., #112, Denver | mrbswineandspirits.com**

GREAT DIVIDE BREWING: Only a few blocks away from Mr. B's. Step up to the bar in the clean and modern tap room, order tasters of world-class Yeti imperial stout variations, grab some food from one of the food trucks perpetually stationed out front, and chat with the bartender about the expansive new facility in the River North neighborhood. **2201 Arapahoe St., Denver | greatdivide.com**

WYNKOOP BREWING COMPANY: Colorado's first brewpub, founded in 1988 by now-Governor John Hickenlooper, is great if you're hungry. Enjoy an upscale take on pub food (try the short rib poutine if you're so inclined). They've recently revamped their brewhouse and pulled back from packaging beer, but the beers are solid, the food is delicious, and the location can't be beat. **1634 18th St., Denver | wynkoop.com**

FRESHCRAFT: Combines a killer tap list and reserve bottle list with a creative kitchen, and you never know what beer "celebrity" you might end up sitting next to. We've found everything from Casey Brewing wild ales to vintage Surly Darkness on tap there (it's busy during GABF week, but the tap takeover events are not-to-be-missed). **1530 Blake St., Denver | freshcraft.com**

EUCLID HALL BAR & KITCHEN: For a tightly curated beer list and food that will challenge and excite you (think pig ears and bone marrow as well as a full lineup of house-made charcuterie), don't miss Euclid Hall. **Larimer Square, 1317 14th St., Denver | euclidhall.com**

COORS FIELD: If you're up for catching a Rockies game, you're in luck—Coors Field has great beer options that span from 30+ craft beers served from the taps of the Rooftop bar to Coors's Sandlot brewery at the eastern corner of the field. With 40+ GABF medals to their name, The Sandlot might be the winningest draft-only brewery in the country. **Coors Field, 2001 Blake St., Denver**

HONORABLE DOWNTOWN MENTIONS: While we wouldn't visit Denver Beer Co. (denverbeerco.com) just for the beer, the location is great, surrounding restaurants such as Colt & Gray are definitely worth a visit, and it's a hopping scene for people watching. Jagged Mountain Brewery (jaggedmountainbrewery.com) went through a tough period with beer we couldn't recommend, but have begun to turn things around under the direction of their new brewer.

DENVER RIVER NORTH AND FIVE POINTS

There's no doubt that some of the most aggressive growth in the Denver beer world is happening on the north side of downtown, in the former industrial buildings of the River North (RiNo) district.

FIRST DRAFT TAPROOM & KITCHEN: Heading north from LoDo, make a stop at First Draft Taproom & Kitchen, and sample from the 40 taps where you pay by the ounce and pour it yourself. The food is delicious and the flexibility in pour size is perfect for craft beer fans who want to sample small amounts of lots of different beers. But ease of service isn't the only selling point—owner Mark Slattery (@DenverBeerGuy on Twitter) is an active part of the craft-beer community and keeps a consistently awesome lineup of the best local breweries and creative, harder-to-find national options. **1309 26th St., Denver | firstdraftdenver.com**

OUR MUTUAL FRIEND BREWING: The cozy contemporary tap room features beers worth checking out—their focus on Colorado-grown ingredients offers a unique angle even if they've backed away from malting their own grain as of late. **2810 Larimer St., Denver | omfbeer.com**

RATIO BEERWORKS: One of the cooler tap rooms we've seen. The indie music references in the beer names (Repeater, Dear You, Domestica) are fun, and the sum of the experience is greater than the individual beers. **2920 Larimer St., Denver | ratiobeerworks.com**

EPIC BREWING COMPANY: Three blocks over, the Denver expansion brewery for Salt Lake City's EPIC Brewing offers a gorgeous modern bar, expansive tap room, and a deep selection of Epic beers on tap. Wood foeders add ambiance and hold sour beer for their rapidly expanding sour program. But if sour isn't your thing, try the highly rated Double Skull dopplebock, the Escape to Colorado IPA, or the exquisite Big Bad Baptist imperial stout. **3001 Walnut St., Denver | epicbrewing.com/locations/denver-brewery-and-tap-room**

SPANGALANG BREWERY: These three former Great Divide employees broke off to do their own thing, but you can taste the discipline and consistency in the beer they make at Spangalang. Their hoppy beers are solid, the stouts are excellent, and the farmhouse-style beers are dry, crisp, and incredibly refreshing. The location might seem a bit rough from the outside, but the beer is worth the trip, and it's a quick trip from downtown via Uber or light rail. **2736 Welton St., Denver | spangalangbrewery.com**

Once you've finished that side of RiNo, venture to the other side of the tracks (the River North district is bisected by a rail yard that makes getting around a bit tricky). Until the city builds a pedestrian bridge, a cab or car-sharing service is your best bet.

MOCKERY BREWING: Newcomer Mockery is making a name for itself with creative beer, a comfortable patio, and a well-designed tap room that showcases its 15-barrel Premier brewhouse. The Oaked Southern Hemisphere Black Pale Ale sounds like a disaster but tastes fantastic, and the Salted Scotch Ale has a malty body but clever dry finish that avoids clichés.

3501 Delgany St., Denver | mockerybrewing.com

GREAT DIVIDE BARREL BAR: Next door, the new Great Divide Barrel Bar recently opened in their huge and gleaming packaging hall. Grab some highly rated barrel-aged Yeti variants, enjoy the furniture and fixtures made from reclaimed barrels, and watch their bottling and canning lines in action.

1812 35th St., Denver | greatdivide.com/tap-rooms

CROOKED STAVE ARTISAN BEER PROJECT: For the ultimate finale in River North, it's essential to stop at the Crooked Stave Taproom at The Source (below left). The mixed-development building is home to restaurants Comida and Acorn, a butcher, a bakery, a coffee roaster, a liquor store, and a design gallery in addition to Denver's temple of sour and wild beer. With the brew system now relocated to the barrel cellar (a few miles away), the tap room has plenty of space for the crowds that line up daily for the 20-plus taps that feature everything from 100 percent *Brett*-fermented saisons to dry-hopped dark sours and fruited petite sours. 3350 Brighton Blvd., Denver | thesourcedenver.com/crooked-stave

NEW BELGIUM THE WOODS: Opening in The Source hotel in 2017, this sour-beer outpost will offer yet another reason to lose an afternoon or evening in RiNo. The 10 bbl brewhouse on the first floor will serve the poolside barrel-aging facility and lounge on the 8th floor, making for one of the most unique sour experiences in the world. 3350 Brighton Blvd., Denver | newbelgium.com/Brewery/TheWoods

DENVER TENNYSON AND HIGHLAND

Denver has pockets of cool neighborhoods all over the city, and Tennyson is one that's definitely worth a visit.

SMALL BATCH LIQUORS: This cozy shop is a great place to pick up hard-to-find bottles from breweries such as Glenwood Springs–based Casey Brewing & Blending or Crooked Stave as well as imported lambic, freshly-canned hoppy beers from Odd 13 and Station 26, and more.

4340 Tennyson St., Denver | smallbatchliquors.com

HOPS & PIE: Grab some pizza from Hops & Pie, a few blocks south, and open up the trapper-keeper beer list to ogle the reserve beers from Crooked Stave, Cascade, Almanac, and others. If you time it right, don't miss one of Hops & Pie's "Littlest Big Wild & Sour Fest" events with kegs of Cantillon, Russian River, Tilquin, The Bruery, Jester King, and more. 3920 Tennyson St., Denver | hopsandpie.com

CALL TO ARMS BREWING COMPANY: Features a beautiful retro-contemporary tap room that opens to the outdoors when the weather is nice (which, being Colorado, is pretty often). While our first visit to the brewery shortly after they opened was not terribly impressive, they've fixed those early issues and are making beer we can now recommend. 4526 Tennyson St., Denver | calltoarmsbrewing.com

HOGSHEAD BREWERY: For an entirely different beer experience, visit Hogshead Brewery farther down Tennyson. Its focus on traditional English-style beers and cask ales is a pleasant change of pace, and the beers are very well-crafted and perfectly served. **4460 W. 29th Ave., Denver I hogsheadbrewery.com**

PROST BREWING: If German beers are your jam, then a visit to Prost Brewing is in order. Their GABF gold medals for Hefeweizen and Keller Pils are proof of high-quality execution. **2540 19th St., Denver I prostbrewing.com**

DENVER CHERRY CREEK AND GLENDALE

It's a harder sell to get visitors to venture out of the Downtown/LoDo/River North area of Denver, but those who do are rewarded with a few real Denver gems.

COPPER KETTLE BREWING: Is located in an otherwise nondescript office and warehouse complex, but since it opened in 2011, it has developed a reputation for well-executed beers such as the Well Bred barrel-aged barleywine and the GABF gold-winning Mexican Chocolate Stout. The tap room (below) regularly offers small-run specialty beers such as rum barrel–aged Pumpkin Porter. **1338 S. Valentia St., #100, Denver I copperkettledenver.com**

COMRADE BREWING: Just down the road, Comrade Brewing has made a huge splash in its first two years of operation, landing on many Colorado critics' best-of lists and earning back to back silver medals at the GABF for the Superdamp fresh hops IPA, and a World Beer Cup gold for chili beer Yellow Fever. Its hoppy beers (Superpower IPA, Putsch Black IPA, Hop Chops DIPA) and expansive but friendly tap room are worth the extra drive from downtown. **7667 E. Iliff Ave., Denver I comradebrewing.com**

THE BULL AND BUSH: If you prefer your beer and pubs English-style and have a thing for kitschy seventies decor, stepping into Bull and Bush (above) is like a time warp back to the first time you walked into a Steak and Ale—except that Bull and Bush has won a dozen medals at the World Beer Cup and GABF since their mid-nineties inception. The beer is fantastic and anything but kitsch. **4700 Cherry Creek Dr. S., Denver | bullandbush.com**

GRAPEVINE WINE & LIQUORS: While in that vicinity, beer hunters will want to take a detour by Grapevine. But don't stop at the cooler doors; ask the staff, then walk back into the cooler for expansive racks of hard-to-find beer. The beer buyers love to have fun with customers, holding beers such as Bourbon County Brand Stout, then putting bottles on the shelves in random places and at random times, making every visit a quasi-Easter-egg hunt. **900 S. Monaco Pkwy., Denver, | facebook.com/GrapevineWineandLiquors**

WASH PARK, PLATT PARK, GOLDEN TRIANGLE

Things are heating up in the neighborhoods south of downtown. Huge apartment and condo developments are reinvigorating former industrial properties, and a number of breweries have moved in along with them.

BLACK PROJECT SPONTANEOUS & WILD ALES: The brewery formerly known as Former Future has now been subsumed by their own wild-ale project. It's all sour beer now as Founders James and Sarah Howat pursue their passion for wild and spontaneous fermentation with a singular focus. Dreamland is delicious, but try Ejector if you love the intersection of acidity and hoppiness—it's bright, funky, and worth seeking out. **1290 S. Broadway, Denver | blackprojectbeer.com**

TRVE BREWING: The most "unique" brewery in Denver (in terms of tap room experience, right) sits in a nondescript block of South Broadway. The black walls, skulls, pentagrams, candles, and doom metal soundtrack immediately tell you that this brewery is unlike just about anything else you've experienced, but the beer itself is remarkable for its contrast to this extreme tap room vibe—sessionable core styles that they continuously work to perfect rather than brewing a succession of one-off specials. The result is a tap room that transcends the metal style and attracts everyone from bearded metalheads to well-dressed business women. **227 Broadway, #101, Denver | trvebrewing.com**

BAERE BREWING: Their brewhouse might be small (a mere 2.5 bbls), but the brewers at Baere have good taste and brew interesting beers in a number of styles. The beers rotate quickly due to the small batch size, but on one recent visit we really enjoyed the American Farmhouse ale, Dry-Hopped Barrel-aged Sour, and Big Hoppy Brown. **320 Broadway, Denver | baerebrewing.com**

STRANGE CRAFT BEER CO: Best-known in Colorado for their grapefruit IPA, Strange Craft has pulled in awards on the national and international stage since 2011. Their Dr. Strangelove barleywine has medaled in both the GABF and World Beer Cup, and their Cherry Kriek won WBC gold in 2014. The flex-space warehouse isn't the most illustrious location to enjoy their beer, but it's the only spot to try their one-barrel pilot batches and specialty firkins. **1330 Zuni St., Denver, | strangecraft.com**

CITY PARK AND STAPLETON

STATION 26 BREWING CO: This old fire station has been repurposed into one of Denver's better breweries (and that's saying a lot). In warmer weather, the rolling front doors open up for a beer garden feel on the front patio, with indie hits on the soundtrack and communal tables for beer drinkers. Beers range from the clean and crisp Colorado Cream Ale to the punchy hops of Juicy Banger IPA, but the best thing they brew is canned and gets decent distribution throughout the front range—the Single Hop IPA series. Single Hop Citra was incredible, Single Hop Chinook was eye opening in its creativity with that humble hops, and variations with Amarillo, Mosaic, and Simcoe have all deftly showcased those hops' flavors. **7045 E. 38th Ave., Denver | station26brewing.com**

FICTION BEER COMPANY: The literary theme is strong here, with a bar built from old books and literary beer references emblazoned on the tables. The beer, however, stands up to the concept with hops, haze, and sour beers being the main attraction.
7101 E. Colfax Ave., Denver | fictionbeer.com

AURORA AND THE AIRPORT

If you're flying into Denver, Aurora is a great stop on the way in from the airport.

DRY DOCK BREWING: Treat yourself to one of Dry Dock Brewing's very well-crafted barrel-aged beers at their South Dock location. It's a testament to the selection available in the Colorado market that these beers last more than a day on store shelves. If the drive is too much, pick up a bottle of Bligh's Barleywine (or any of the Signature Series beers). You won't be disappointed. **Hampden Villa, 15120 E. Hampden Ave., Aurora | drydockbrewing.com/south-dock**

NEW BELGIUM HUB: In Denver International Airport (below). In addition to brewery standards such as Fat Tire and 1554, the rotating tap has been known to dispense La Folie from time to time. Hub's no-frills food menu features sandwiches, chicken, and waffles. Denver's underground train makes transferring between concourses fast and convenient, so even Concourse C passengers can easily get over to Hub. But be ready for a walk—Hub is located at the farthest end of Concourse B. **Denver International Airport, Concourse B | flydenver.com/enjoy_relax/dine/new-belgium-hub**

LAKEWOOD, LITTLETON, HIGHLANDS RANCH

FARMHOUSE AT BRECKENRIDGE BREWERY: No trip to Denver would be complete without a visit to Breckenridge Brewery, and the new-ish farmhouse brewery in Littleton is a beer sight to behold. They spared no expense in constructing this showpiece brewery, and it's a

great place to enjoy a pint of the Vanilla Porter or 72 Imperial Chocolate Stout. Don't hesitate to grab a bite from the restaurant while there—the food is first rate and getting a table on weekend evenings can pose a challenge due to high demand, but there's plenty of beer to drink while you wait. **2990 Brewery Ln., Littleton | breckbrewfarmhouse.com**

MILE HIGH WINES & SPIRITS: This Lakewood liquor store is worth the drive for its extensive selection of hard-to-find bottles. Its "Notes from the Cooler" blog noting new arrivals has fallen off since former beer buyer André DiMattia left to join Crooked Stave's distribution arm, but its Facebook feed is quickly updated as new beers arrive. **435 S. Vance St., Lakewood | milehighwineandspirits.com**

LIVING THE DREAM BREWING: Colorado outdoors is the theme for this suburban Highlands Ranch warehouse brewery specializing in hops and stouts. If you're down in the area visiting Breckenridge, make a stop here and hope they're pouring some of the barrel-aged projects they've started releasing ... you won't be disappointed. **12305 N. Dumont Wy., Littleton | livingthedreambrewing.com**

GOLDEN

Coors's hometown is also home to a handful of creative craft brewers.

CANNONBALL CREEK BREWING: Truly a reason to hoof it out to Golden, Cannonball Creek (above) is brewing some of the most interesting and exciting hoppy beers in all of Colorado. Their Project Alpha series focuses on hops flavors more than bitterness, and their hoppy beers are so popular (and sell so well at the brewery itself) that they don't need to distribute outside of special occasions. Skip the Belgian-style beers while you're there (you can find better iterations of those elsewhere) but the stouts don't disappoint. **393 Washington Ave., Golden | cannonballcreekbrewing.com**

BARRELS & BOTTLES BREWERY: This brewpub serves its own beer side-by-side with some of the best from breweries around Colorado and the world, and their Orange Creamsicle Blonde ale can certainly hold its own. The menu is simple and fine for lunch, but those looking for more of a meal might want to move on after a few rounds. **600 12th St., #160, Golden | barrelsbottles.com**

COORS: We're not going to judge if you decide to take the tour of one of the largest breweries in the world. Honestly. **Ford St., Golden | visitgolden .com/coors-brewery**

BOULDER

Denver may be the capital of brewing in Colorado, but Boulder (and its close neighbor Longmont) are, arguably, its spiritual center. Home to the Brewers Association, the American Homebrewers Association, and Colorado's first craft brewery, the Boulder area has a long history of leading and inspiring brewers both inside and outside of the state.

AVERY BREWING COMPANY: If you drink craft beer at all, it's almost certain you've heard the name Avery Brewing at least once. These Boulder-area stalwarts have been doing their thing for 20+ years now and have done plenty of pioneering work in barrel-aging and sour-beer fermentation, but most of that history was spent in an unassuming (and parking-challenged) business park lovingly named "the alley." Last year, Avery built their dream brewery just outside of Boulder in Gunbarrel, and the gleaming temple of the brewer's craft is a must-visit. If your goal is a meal, book a reservation in advance on Open Table—the limited space in the upstairs dining room gets booked fast, and the alternative is often a two-hour wait for a table. But the good news is the kitchen is fantastic, and you won't regret it. If you do have to wait, grab a beer from the bar and stroll through the raised walkways on the self-guided tour overlooking the brewery. Before you leave, check out the cold cases across from the hostess stand—Avery is notorious for stocking it with vintage bottles from their barrel-aged series. **4910 Nautilus Ct., Boulder | averybrewing.com**

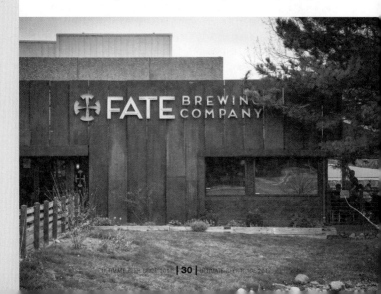

UPSLOPE BREWING: Back in Boulder proper, a visit to one of the Upslope Brewing locations should be next on your list. The original brewery on Lee Hill Road now handles small and specialty batches, while the main production brewery in Flatiron Park pumps out larger volumes of cans, but either offers a deep tap list of beers you won't find on store shelves. If you visit the Flatiron Park location on a Friday, pop into White Labs' Colorado office next door and sample some of the test batches brewed with their range of brewer's yeast. **1501 Lee Hill / 1898 S. Flatiron Ct., Boulder | upslopebrewing.com**

FATE BREWING COMPANY: Minutes away is Fate (left)—a clean, modern, stylishly appointed brewpub just up Arapahoe Road. It's perpetually busy, thanks to a winning combination of solid beer and creative menu. They're most known for lighter styles, such as their Laimas Kölsch (2014 GABF gold medal winner) and Uror Gose, and their brewing is understandably focused on lighter styles that pair well with meals. **1600 38th St., Boulder | fatebrewingcompany.com**

BRU HANDBUILT ALES & EATS: brews ingredient-focused beers with an emphasis on spices, herbs, roots, and unexpected adjuncts. The beers mesh beautifully with the restaurant side of the business, and the food and beer menus change constantly to incorporate ingredients that are seasonally and locally available. Some of the beer goes to BRU's house vinegar, and the spent grains are used to bake bread and to feed local pigs—they then purchase the pigs fed with their grains to serve in the restaurant. Fourteen taps are available, and only five of those are year-round beers, so you can expect the unexpected at BRU. **5290 Arapahoe Rd., Boulder | bruboulder.com**

BACKCOUNTRY PIZZA & TAP HOUSE: For a more casual menu and an absolutely stunning tap and bottle list, make your next stop at Backcountry Pizza (above). Owner John Fayman is a true beer lover, an investor in Wyoming's Melvin Brewing, and the force behind Denver's first sour-beer bar, Goed Zuur. It's no surprise, then, that the 68t taps include beers you won't find anywhere else in Colorado or that the bottle list includes deep sour selections from Russian River, Jolly Pumpkin, Jester King, Crooked Stave, and a handful of Belgium's best. **2319 Arapahoe Ave., Boulder | backcountry | pizzaandtaphouse.com**

BOULDER BEER: If history is your thing, Colorado's first craft brewery, Boulder Beer, is worth a stop. Grab a pint of Shake Chocolate Porter or Hazed Hoppy Session Ale (which was hazy long before haze was cool again), a quick bite from the pub-centric menu, and enjoy one of the 300 days of sunshine that Colorado has to offer. **2880 Wilderness Pl., Boulder | boulderbeer.com**

BOHEMIAN BIERGARTEN: The Czech beer-hall experience is on point at this Boulder favorite. From classic drafts to an authentic menu, it's a fun spot for an evening with friends where beer is the lubricant for socializing. **2017 13th St., Boulder | bohemianbiergarten.com**

HAZEL'S BEVERAGE WORLD: If you're looking for bottles to take back home, do yourself a favor and first check Hazel's. Those visiting from more beer-challenged states might be taken aback upon stepping into Hazel's—it's the size of a grocery store and even features a P-51 Mustang hanging from the rafters. Wednesdays and Thursdays are great days to shop—the very rare releases go quickly once they make it onto the store shelves. **1955 28th St., Boulder | hazelsboulder.com**

REDSTONE MEADERY: Rooted in the ideals of traditional meaderies, Redstone Meadery (right) sticks to the "philosophy of mead." They avoid sulfites and instead use locally sourced honey, which is a natural preservative and also influences the flavor, depending on where the bees have spent their time. Instead of cork, they use swing-top bottles that offer a longer shelf life. Stop by for a free half-hour tour, which includes a tasting for those who are 21 and older. Stick around for a while on a Saturday between November and April, and you can be treated to a live music show. **4700 Pearl St., Unit 2A, Boulder | redstonemeadery.com**

LIQUOR MART: If you're doing the rounds, Liquor Mart is similarly scaled to Hazel's with door after door full of local and regional craft beer and worth a visit. **1750 15th St., Boulder | liquormart.com/beer**

WHOLE FOODS MARKET: Colorado law only allows companies to own a single retail beer, wine, and liquor location, so every store in the entire state is a one-off (there are no chains). However, even the big grocery chains have taken advantage of their legal right to operate a single liquor store, and Whole Foods located theirs in Boulder. **Crossroad Commons, 2905 Pearl St., Boulder | wholefoodsmarket.com/stores/boulder**

MOUNTAIN SUN PUB & BREWERY: is a laidback brewpub where locals, regulars, families, and visiting beer geeks can enjoy their house beers, from the Colorado Kind Ale (amber ale hopped with Cascade) to the Isadore Java Porter (brewed with "a generous amount of coffee"). For food, there is a solid selection of vegetarian offerings, including the outstanding tempeh Reuben sandwich and a hefty Boulder burrito. And service is notoriously friendly. Ten GABF medals over the years can't be wrong. **1535 Pearl St., Boulder | mountainsunpub.com**

HONORABLE MENTION: If you're making a longer day of it, there are plenty of other solid beer locations in Boulder—Finkel & Garf's (finkeland garf.com) mid-century mod tap room is just down the road from Avery;

West Flanders (wfbrews.com) offers just-okay beer from a phenomenal location on the Pearl Street mall; the Sundown Saloon (facebook.com/The-Sundown-Saloon) on Pearl Street is known for cheap pitchers and college kids but keeps an impressive bottle list that you'd never expect to see; Twisted Pine Brewing (twistedpinebrewing.com) will melt your face off with their Ghost Face Killah chile beer; the West End Tavern (thewestendtavern.com) offers a fantastic tap list and incredible pub fare to go with it; and Sanitas Brewing (sanitasbrewing.com) is growing their reputation for creative and well-crafted beers.

NIWOT

As you head from Boulder toward Longmont, make a point to stop in the tiny town of Niwot for not one but two quality breweries.

BOOTSTRAP BREWING: Grab a pint of their Insane Rush IPA and kick back on the outdoor patio. If you dig it, grab some cans of Insane Rush or Stick's Pale Ale to go—the packaging is as gorgeous as the beer is good.
6778 N. 79th St., Niwot, I bootstrapbrewing.com

POWDER KEG: Hope they have one of their fruited wild ales available (they're fantastic), but if not, they offer a wide selection of their own beers in addition to a healthy tap list of guest beers from folks such as Perennial, Firestone Walker, Melvin, and more. **101 2nd Ave. Niwot I**

powderkegbrewingcompany.com

LYONS

If beer is your goal, then there's only a single reason to go to Lyons (other than the fantastic mountain biking at Hall Ranch and our favorite bike shop on the planet, Redstone Cycles)...

ORIGINAL OSKAR BLUES BREWPUB: Before the private equity investment and acquisitions, it all started right there. If you're a fan of the brand, it's a necessary pilgrimage. **303 Main St., Lyons | oskarblues.com**

LONGMONT

The Oskar Blues "empire" extends to neighboring Longmont, and they own and operate no fewer than four separate locations here...

OSKAR BLUES' TASTY WEASEL TAP ROOM: With skeeball lanes that overlook one of their canning lines at the main Oskar Blues brewery (below) and an extensive array of taproom-only beers, it's a must-visit for OB fans. Think dry-hopped Dale's Pale Ale or barrel-aged Old Chub with a touch of rock 'n' roll and typical Oskar Blues swagger. **1800 Pike Rd., Longmont | facebook.com/The-Tasty-Weasel**

OSKAR BLUES' CHUBURGER: For casual burgers with your beer, head over and order a Berk Burger—the ground pork patty, bacon, caramelized onions, and blue-cheese butter are exquisite in their excess. An array of OB beers are available on tap and in cans, as well as guest beers from other Colorado breweries. **1225 Ken Pratt Blvd., Longmont | oskarbluesfooderies.com/chuburger**

OSKAR BLUES' HOMEMADE LIQUIDS & SOLIDS: Great for a sit-down Southern-style meal, OB's Homemade Liquids & Solids offers 40-something taps to go along with the food, and it's again not just Oskar Blues beer. Yes, that's the one with the painted silo attached to it, so you just can't miss it. **1555 S. Hover Rd., Longmont | oskarbluesfooderies.com/home-made-liquids-and-solids**

OSKAR BLUES' CYCLHOPS MEXICAN BIKE CANTINA: With street tacos, more beer, margaritas, and their very own bike shop, this is one of the more unique dining experiences in Longmont and a great spot to visit if you're hanging with non-beer-drinking friends. **600 S. Airport Rd., Longmont |** **oskarbluesfooderies.com/cyclhops**

LEFT HAND BREWING: Grab a pint of Nitro Milk Stout (rated a 97 by *CB&B Magazine)* from the source. This employee-owned brewery loves to have fun and puts on great festivals just about every other month—from their Hops and Handrails rail jam in March to Nitrofest every November. The tap room is comfortable in a Colorado-meets-English-pub sort of way, and it's a great spot to try some of their new explorations into hoppy beers while getting your fill of their tremendously popular (and delicious) stouts. **1265 Boston Ave., Longmont | lefthandbrewing.com**

WIBBY BREWING: (above) One of the newest additions to the Longmont brewing scene is focused solely on lager brewing, and their IPL and Lightshine Helles (along with their cool open industrial tap room) are worth the visit. **209 Emery St., Longmont | wibbybrewing.com**

WYATT'S WET GOODS: If bottles are your thing, then make a stop by Wyatt's and stock up from their deep selection of local and international bottles and cans. **250 S. Hover Rd., Longmont | wyattswetgoods.com**

GROßEN BART: They take their beards seriously at Großen Bart (German for "big beard"), as evidenced by the mustache-shaped taster trays and glassware printed with beard styles, but our favorite thing on their menu is the sour beers. **1025 Delaware Ave., Longmont | grossenbart.com**

PARRY'S PIZZA: This beer-centric spot has just opened a fourth location around the corner from Wyatt's with 100 taps that focus on really great Colorado beer. **1232 S. Hover Rd., #100, Longmont | parryspizza.com/longmont**

HONORABLE MENTION: if you're in the mood for a Longmont classic, a stop at The Pumphouse Brewery (pumphousebrewery.com) will net you some solid pub food and average in-house beers, but their guest taps are always killer.

LAFAYETTE

This growing beer destination punches above its weight class with a couple breweries making statewide waves despite their small-town origins.

THE POST BREWING: (below right) Normally, you hear "restaurant group" and cringe at the thought of bland beer, but this brewery owned by Big Red F restaurants did it right by recruiting Bryan Selders, former Dogfish Head brewmaster, and setting him loose to build a brewhouse and brew beer that complements their culinary offerings. While Selders was known for genre-defying beers at Dogfish Head, he's gone the other direction at The Post, refining simple, sessionable beers into an immaculately crafted lineup. The 4.5 percent ABV Howdy Beer Pilsner is tight, crisp, and palate cleansing, while the 6 percent ABV Cul-de-Sac oatmeal stout is one of the tastiest you will ever have the pleasure of drinking. The most fun way to enjoy the beers is in the 21+ Elkhorn Room in the back—the ersatz Elk or Moose "lodge" with padded leather barstools and trophies mounted on the walls is kitschy, but the beer is the absolute truth. **105 W. Emma St., Lafayette | postbrewing.com**

ODD 13 BREWING: They've watched their star rise in 2016 on the strength of very creative, hazy, hoppy beers such as their Codename: Superfan IPA. A new separate production brewery with a 30 bbl brewhouse joins the 10 bbl brewhouse at the taproom, allowing them to pump out cans in greater volume to meet the demand for those soft and fluffy IPAs that are in short supply in the state. But don't overlook their sour beers while drinking the hops—they're equally committed to brewing interesting sours with clever techniques. **301 E. Simpson St., Lafayette | odd13brewing.com**

LIQUID MECHANICS BREWING COMPANY: Grab a glass of their Peanut Butter Porter or GABF medal-winning Altbier before heading off to your next stop. **297 US-287, #100, Lafayette | liquidmechanicsbrewing.com**

ERIE

THE OLD MINE: This combination of cidery and craft-beer bar offers a light menu of pizzas and smoked meats. With a dozen of their own various ciders on tap—everything from dry-hopped to blueberry to barrel-aged—plus another dozen craft beers with a strong leaning toward vintage sours and stouts, it's a great place to visit if you're traveling with someone who doesn't love beer quite as much as you. Take a peek at the bottle list while you're there—they've been known to put back some Belgian gems. **500 Briggs St., Erie | theoldmine.com**

LOVELAND AND BERTHOUD

CITY STAR BREWING: City Star might be the best thing to ever come out of the (mostly) bedroom community of Berthoud. Their medal-winning Bandit Brown ale is a knockout, and their Night Watchman stout packs a lot of smooth flavor into a sessionable package. The rustic tap room evokes the Wild West, so cozy up to the bar or grab a table and enjoy a few. **321 Mountain Ave., Berthoud | citystarbrewing.com**

VERBOTEN BREWING: The hip new downtown Loveland brewery and tap room are a huge step up over Verboten's former characterless strip warehouse location, and the digs now do justice to the creatively designed and well-executed brews they've been pumping out for a few years. Equally adept at hoppy beers such as Stand Up Philosopher DIPA and malty faves such as Pure Imagination stout (rated 96 by *CB&B Magazine*), their small scale barrel-aging program has also turned out some really nice beers.

127 E. 5th St., Loveland | verbotenbrewing.com

LOVELAND ALEWORKS: About a block away from Verboten on 4th Street, Loveland Aleworks has turned a historic downtown storefront into a gorgeous tap room and brewery. Across the board, the beers are solid, but we find ourselves gravitating to the various fruited American sour beers when we visit. It makes a great stop on a downtown Loveland beer crawl.

118 W. 4th St., Loveland | lovelandaleworks.com

LAUREATE PUBLICK HOUSE: The cousin bar of Fort Collins's The Forge, The Laureate adds a creative bar menu on top of the expected killer tap list, and the result is a third must-visit spot for beer fans in Loveland.

548 N. Lincoln Ave., Loveland, | laureatepub.com

GRIMM BROTHERS BREWHOUSE: Carving out a niche with German-style lagers isn't so easy in the world of craft beer, and Grimm Brothers Brewhouse launched with this focus years before craft lagers became cool again. Over the years, they've honed their process and begun canning, making these balanced, drinkable, and flavorful lagers ubiquitous across northern Colorado. The tap room itself is a great spot to grab limited release and pilot batches while noshing on fare from the many food trucks that park out front.

623 Denver Ave., Loveland | grimmbrosbrewhouse.com

LIQUOR MAX: This warehouse-sized liquor store completed a huge expansion of its craft beer aisles, and now offers 20+ doors full of well-curated craft offerings. If you're looking for obscure and amazing European releases or a deep dive into the best that local breweries have to offer, you won't be disappointed. **1497 E. Eisenhower Blvd., Loveland | liquormax.net**

GREELEY AND WINDSOR

WELDWERKS BREWING: *USA Today* voted them top new brewery in 2016, and for good reason—their New England-style IPA Juicy Bits has been called "The best IPA in Colorado" by a few critics, and their barrel-aged stout, Medianoche, had 350+ beer fans lined up for the limited brewery release. But you don't have to seek out the rare stuff to enjoy their beer, and we recommend everything from their mainline Steambarrel IPA to their fruited Goses and Berliner-style Weisse beers.
508 8th Ave., Greeley | weldwerksbrewing.com

WILEY ROOTS BREWING: For a working-class agriculture-driven city like Greeley to have one great craft brewery is impressive, but the fact that they have two should make it a stop on any Colorado beercation. Wiley Roots might not be riding the same hype wave as Weldwerks, but their sour beers are incredible and their Super 77 American Wheat has won both bronze and gold medals at the GABF, proving they're no fluke.
625 3rd St., Greeley | wileyroots.com

HIGH HOPS BREWERY: First there was the Windsor Gardener garden shop, then they started cultivating and selling hops. Eventually, they decided to start brewing with those hops they grew, and the rest is history. The tap room gets a bit warm in the summer due to the connecting greenhouse, but drinking beer on the patio overlooking their hops field is a fun and fairly unique experience in Colorado. **6461 CO-392, Windsor | highhopsbrewery.com**

FORT COLLINS

NEW BELGIUM: This Fort Collins stalwart needs little introduction—you'd be hard pressed to find a craft-beer drinker who isn't familiar with their flagship Fat Tire Ale. But a recent tap room expansion that added additional beer service locations and replaced a small parking lot with a huge lawn for drinking visitors has made the brewery experience even better. We've toured hundreds and hundreds of breweries over the years and can say (without a doubt) that the New Belgium tour experience is one of the absolute best. Whip-smart and funny tour guides, lots of free beer at stops throughout the tour, the chance to spend time among the 60+ foeders in their sour-beer hall, and a chance to slide down the spiral slide at the end of the tour make it fun, irreverent, and educational. It's a must-visit on any Colorado itinerary. If hops are your thing, then try their limited-release Hop Kitchen beers. If you're into sour beer, then the tap room usually offers ultra-limited releases such as Felix (their blonde sour-base beer) aged in Leopold fruit whiskey barrels. And if Belgian-style beers are your thing, then you're really in luck, because their Abbey and Tripel beers are some of the best and most-overlooked examples of the styles brewed in the United States. **500 Linden St., Fort Collins | newbelgium.com**

ODELL BREWING COMPANY: A true brewers' brewery, Odell's focus on experimentation, cutting-edge technique, and some of the best raw materials procurement in the business gives their beer a unique advantage in the competitive Colorado market. The fact that they've won medals in so many different styles—from their flagship 90 Shilling to Easy Street Wheat to 5 Barrel Pale Ale to Odell IPA to sour fruit beer Friek—is evidence of their versatility. The tap room itself is a site to behold—order from the registers as you walk in, open a tab, grab your beer from the bar behind the registers, and find a spot on the gorgeous sprawling patio or at the many communal tables inside. On weekend afternoons it's tough to find a seat, as locals and visitors alike soak up the Colorado sun while enjoying their classics as well as the frequent pilot beers and one-offs. **800 E. Lincoln Ave., Fort Collins | odellbrewing.com**

FUNKWERKS: (above) A more intimate experience than the big two breweries in Fort Collins, Funkwerks still holds its own in the beer department even if the tap room is a tenth the size! Their singular focus on Belgian-style beers driven by their immaculately crafted Saison means they won't be everything to everyone, but to our palates theirs is consistently one of the best brewed saisons in the United States. Their expansion in sour beer with the Provincial series has netted more delicious and accessible options for beer fans, and their extremely limited barrel-aged saisons regularly top critics best-of-lists. **1900 E. Lincoln Ave., Fort Collins | funkwerks.com**

ZWEI BREWING: The brewery is fairly new, but the brewers behind it have a long history of brewing in Fort Collins. Their lagers are some of the best in the state. **4612 S. Mason St., #120, Fort Collins | zweibrewing.com**

TAP AND HANDLE: (below) With 74 taps and an extensive bottle list, Tap and Handle is a beer-geek's beer bar without the pretension. The bar keeps 20+ hoppy beers on tap at any given time (from Melvin 2x4 to La Cumbre Project Dank and Boneyard RPM and Notorious), as well as 15+ sour beers, vintage bottles from Avery, Jester King, Tilquin and more, plus straightforward pub fare from the full kitchen. If the weather's nice, grab a seat on the patio next to one of the fire pits. **307 S. College Ave., Fort Collins | tapandhandle.com**

HORSE & DRAGON BREWING COMPANY: A local favorite, Horse & Dragon has built their following on a reputation for well-made beers and friendly service. They don't package, so draft (at local beer bars or their tap room) is the only way to experience it. Their Sad Panda coffee stout is delicious, the Almost Summer golden ale is a crushable classic, and the Maracuyá IPA will fulfill all your fruit IPA desires. **124 Racquette Dr., Fort Collins | horseanddragonbrewing.com**

EQUINOX BREWING: Another favorite local hangout, Equinox sells beer only to places it can deliver to via bike. As a result, most of what they brew is sold over the bar at their tap room, and that's the best place to sample their classic GABF gold medal-winning beers. Space Ghost IPA is beloved, and their cask engine beers never disappoint. **133 Remington St., Fort Collins | equinoxbrewing.com**

THE MAYOR OF OLD TOWN: With 100 taps and a clean, modern interior, The Mayor is a great place to sample beers from many of the best breweries in northern Colorado. If you can't find something on the menu you love, you're not looking hard enough. **632 S. Mason St., Fort Collins | themayorofoldtown.com**

THE FORGE PUBLICK HOUSE: Tucked away in an alley on the north side of Old Town, The Forge is romantically old-school. Cash-only, they feature two bars with different beers on tap at each, and the list is always well-curated. From a design perspective, there might not be another bar in northern Colorado with as much character (the cover of this book was shot at The Forge). **232 Walnut St., Fort Collins | facebook.com/The-Forge-Publick-House**

ESTES PARK

THE BARREL: This seasonal beer garden is the best new addition to Estes Park in years. The bar is built from a repurposed shipping container and seating is all open-air, while the tap list rotates quickly through a mix of top local beers and out-of-state favorites. **116 E. Elkhorn Ave., Estes Park | thebarrel.beer**

VAIL AND BEAVER CREEK

BONFIRE BREWING: welcomes friendly four-legged friends and their humans for beers inside and on the patio (outdoor bonfire included). **127 W. 2nd St., Eagle | bonfirebrewing.com**

CRAZY MOUNTAIN: Much of their production has now been shifted to the former Breckenridge location in Denver that they took over, but the tap room at the original location in Edwards is still one of the best places to enjoy their beer. Grab a Mountain Livin' pale ale or if you're in the mood for a big beer at high altitude, order a Lawyers, Guns, and Money barleywine. **439 Edwards Access Rd. B-102, Edwards | crazymountainbrewery.com**

WEST VAIL LIQUOR MART: If you're visiting and looking for the best place to pick up some great beer at reasonable prices, look no further. **West Vail Mall, 2151 N. Frontage Rd. W., Vail | westvail.com**

FRISCO, BRECKENRIDGE, AND BUENA VISTA

BASECAMP WINES AND SPIRITS: If you're driving in to Breckenridge for a ski weekend, make sure to stop by Basecamp in Frisco on your way in to stock up, as the selection in Breck itself leaves something to be desired. **223 Lusher Ct., #1, Frisco | basecampliquors.com**

THE JAILHOUSE CRAFT BEER BAR: Opened in summer 2016 by former Crooked Stave staffer Sarah Haughey, this destination bar—built in the former jail in Buena Visita—has the type of tap and bottle list you'd expect from an owner so connected to the beer scene. Special kegs from Denver's Comrade Brewing, Glenwood Springs's Casey Brewing & Blending, and more cement a tap lineup sure to please even the most hardened beer geek. **412 E. Main St., Buena Vista | thejailhousebv.com**

SALIDA, PONCHA SPRINGS, AND PAGOSA SPRINGS

ELEVATION BEER COMPANY: Delicious and creative beers, a rustic and cool taproom, and the perfect location for a post-ride beer after riding the Monarch Crest Trail make Elevation Beer Coompany a must-visit when in the area. We love their Oil Man bourbon barrel–aged stout, their Raspberry Gulch saison, their Senorita horchata-inspired porter, and pretty much everything else they brew, too.

115 Pahlone Pkwy., Poncha Springs | elevationbeerco.com

PAGOSA BREWING & GRILL: Grab a pint of Peanut Butter Cup Stout, order from their full menu, and enjoy a solid meal with great beer.

118 N. Pagosa Blvd., Pagosa Springs | pagosabrewing.com

GLENWOOD SPRINGS, CARBONDALE, AND ASPEN

CASEY BREWING & BLENDING: (right) A niche brewery that only releas-es barrel-fermented mixed-culture beers, their fermentation process uses *Saccharomyces, Brettanomyces,* and lactic acid bacterias, and the beers are unfiltered and bottle conditioned. Only Colorado-grown fruit is used in the brews, including heirloom fruits that are purchased in smaller batches from Colorado's Western Slope. Because they rely on the growers' crop availability, availability of certain brews will vary from month to month and year to year. The batches are small, which means they don't have a tasting room that's open every day. To get in on a tasting at the brewery, you will need to buy a ticket for one of their monthly release parties.

3421 Grand Ave., Glenwood Springs | caseybrewing.com

ASPEN BREWING: Real estate in Aspen is some of the priciest anywhere, so the sheer act of operating a brewery and tap room there isn't cheap. Thankfully, Aspen's brewers have pulled down the medals (including World Beer Cup Gold for their saison in 2014), and the crowds have followed. Their cozy second floor tap room in downtown is a great spot to try their Independence Pass IPA or 10th Mountain Stout, and the outdoor patio overlooking the front side of the resort is a great place to hang any time of the year. **304 E. Hopkins Ave,. Aspen | aspenbrewingcompany.com**

DURANGO, TELLURIDE, AND SILVERTON

SKA BREWING: Down in tiny Durango, the folks from Ska Brewing have been picking it up since 1995—they've lasted longer than most of the bands from that era that inspired them to name the brewery after a musical genre. Their Modus Hoperandi IPA (and the orange peel–infused Modus Mandarina version) are classics, and their seasonal stouts such as Autumnal Molé and Estival Cream stout are unique standouts. With the opening of their small-scale test brewery (branded as Mod Brewing), there's even more reason to visit. **225 Girard St., Durango | skabrewing.com**

TELLURIDE BREWING COMPANY: There must be something in that mountain water. Telluride's Face Down Brown ale has, of late, won gold everywhere—two GABF golds, one World Beer Cup gold—and it will take only one sip for you to understand why. The tap room is small and tucked intimately among the fermentors, giving you an up-close and personal view of how the magic happens. **156 Society Dr., Telluride | telluridebrewingco.com**

COLORADO BOY BREWERY & PUB: Located across from the factory that fabricates the Grammy Awards, Colorado Boy offers the quintessential comfort food that skiers crave after a day on Silverton Mountain: hand-crafted session ales and pizzas. **602 Clinton St., Ridgway | coloradoboy.com**

GRAND JUNCTION AND FRUITA

KANNAH CREEK BREWING: While they've won plenty of awards with traditional-style beers such as their English-style Standing Wave pale ale, Kannah Creek isn't resting on their laurels and has even begun to dip their toe into the world of tart and sour beers. Their brewpub in Grand Junction is where it all began, but they also serve food at their Edgewater production brewery and the newly opened Kannah West out in mountain-biking mecca Fruita, Colorado. **1960 N. 12th St., Grand Junction / 456 Kokopelli Dr., Fruita | kannahcreekbrewingco.com**

ROCKSLIDE BREWERY AND RESTAURANT: Brewers we trust have called Rockslide Head Brewer Zorba Proteau one of the best brewers in Colorado—no small praise given the wealth of great brewers in the state. The beer lineup is focused on session-strength beers that pair well with their brewpub menu, and Proteau is especially strong with hops. **401 Main St., Grand Junction | rockslidebrewpub.com**

COLORADO SPRINGS

TRINITY BREWING: Artisinal saisons and Belgian-style sour beers are Trinity's specialty and should be the focus of any visit. Try the Seven Day Sour, Red Swing Line, Super Juice Solution, and TPS Report (don't be put off by the beer names from the movie *Office Space*—the beers themselves are much less kitschy than their names). The food menu has a variety of bar food, small plates, burgers, and bowls, including a kids menu, as well as some vegan and vegetarian selections, too. **1466 Garden of the Gods Rd., Colorado Springs | trinitybrew.com**

VETERANS LIQUOR: You'd never suspect from their unassuming storefront that a beer-lover's Shangri-La lies within. **3630 Austin Bluffs Pkwy., Colorado Springs | facebook.com/VeteransWine**

BREWER'S REPUBLIC: After hiking all day at Garden of the Gods, it's time to take a load off, have some great food, and, of course, great beer. With 20 craft beers on tap, pizza, and pub fare, this is the place to be. The décor is a bit hipster-ish, with cozy couches and tap handles hanging from the ceiling. Trivia night is a big deal here, so if you've got what it takes, be sure to get in on that, too! **112 N Nevada Ave., Colorado Springs | brewersrep.com**

BRISTOL BREWING COMPANY: What used to be an elementary school found new life in a brewery. We recommend the Laughing Lab, their 9-time GABF winning Scottish Ale, and Winter Warlock Oatmeal Stout. A full-service kitchen is on-site and serves up bar food, sandwiches, and salads. An outdoor patio is the perfect place to play games, and it's dog-friendly! Tours are available only by appointment, so you'll want to call ahead. **1604 S. Cascade Ave., Colorado Springs | bristolbrewing.com**

PHANTOM CANYON BREWING COMPANY: We're big fans of the cask ales at Phantom Canyon, and the kitchen holds its own with quality pub fare. Happy hour is particularly good, with $2.75 pints of their house beers. **2 East Pikes Peak Ave., Colorado Springs | phantomcanyon.com**

COALTRAIN WINE & LIQUOR: This is the place to go when you're looking for an extraordinary selection of beers from all over the world—they've got walls full of special bottles and a knowledgeable staff to help out if you're not sure what to get. **330 W Uintah St., Colorado Springs | coaltrainwine.com**

PIKES PEAK BREWING COMPANY: Sure, the inside of the taproom is stylish, but the views from the outdoor seating areas are outstanding, with views of snow-capped mountains and sky that goes on forever. Live music is sometimes on-site, and food trucks are there on a regular basis, but they do offer a small food menu. They have rotating taps that feature flagships, seasonals, and private reserve beers, as well as wines. As for the beers, we recommend the Elephant Rock IPA, the Summit House Stout, Incline Imperial IPA, and Penrose Private Reserve No. 1302. **1756 Lake Woodmoor Dr., Monument | pikespeakbrewing.com**

MANITOU BREWING COMPANY: It may be small, but it's nabbed a few World Beer Cup medals for its inspired beers. Their High Ground IPA took silver, and its IBU is calculated around 125. Cerise Mousseux Noveau also took silver and uses a combination of beer-brewing and wine-making techniques, and has a touch of *Lacto*. A well-thought food menu has all the favorites as well as vegetarian and gluten-free options. The outdoor patio is a cozy, whimsical setting that's open to dogs. **725 Manitou Ave., Manitou Springs | manitou-brewing.com**

PARADOX BEER: Yeast runs wild at Paradox, where every one of their beers is barrel aged and bottle conditioned, and the specialty is wild and sour beers. Some of our recommendations include Skully Barrel No. 30 (Salty Melons), Skully Barrel No. 25 (Salted Sumac Sour), and Skully Barrel No. 26 (Mango Chili Sour). But really, there is something for every taste here. The tasting room is open select days of the week, and food is provided by McGinty's Wood Oven Pub. **10 Buffalo Ct., Divide | paradoxbeercompany.com**

NEW MEXICO

The desert Southwest is a hotbed of creative brewing, as Albuquerque and Santa Fe have long supported those with a vision of what's possible beyond what currently exists. Whether celebrating historical styles or pushing the boundaries of hops flavors, New Mexico's brewers have made, and continue to make, a strong mark on the world of brewing.

BEST SPOTS FOR OLD SCHOOL BEER STYLES

Chama River has received numerous accolades for their renditions of Pilsners and other Czech- and German-style beers.

BEST SPOTS FOR NEW SCHOOL BEER STYLES

La Cumbre Brewing's (right) progressive approach to exploring hops-forward beers along with their embrace of diverse styles like gose make it a great place to taste the future of craft beer; Marble Brewery's explorations with *Brett* are both old and new again.

BEST SPOTS TO ENJOY A MEAL WITH YOUR BEER

Joseph's of Santa Fe has the upper hand here as they're restaurant first and beer spot second, but the food and service are truly special and a must-experience in Santa Fe.

MOST STYLISH TAPROOMS AND BARS

The roof deck guarantees that Marble Brewery is tops in this category—nothing beats a New Mexico sunset as viewed from a table on the roof deck with a cold beer in hand.

MOST AWARD-WINNING BREWERIES

Canteen (formerly Il Vicino) leads the way with a dozen GABF medals, but Marble Brewery and Chama River aren't far behind.

BEST UNIQUE BEER EXPERIENCE

Try Enchanted Circle's beer brewed only with wild hops foraged from the canyons and forests around them in Angel Fire.

ALBUQUERQUE

NEW MEXICO

LA CUMBRE BREWING: There's something for just about everybody at La Cumbre, which serves up 8 year-round beers and 5 special releases at a time. If you're in the mood for a Hefe, lager, IPA, stout, amber, or red, they've pretty much got you covered, and with 4 Great American Beer Festival wins under their belt, it's obvious they've got a lot to brag about. Seasonal releases might include a fruit beer or barrel-aged brew, or a twist on an old classic. Head over to the tap room seven days a week and order a flight, grab a plate from the food truck, and listen to some live music (if you're there on a Saturday) while playing pool or foosball. And don't forget to grab some cans to go on your way out. **3313 Girard NE, Albuquerque I lacumbrebrewing.com**

MARBLE BREWERY: The brewery is actually two locations: ABQ Downtown, and ABQ Westside. They offer a diverse cast of beers, with 8 Great American Beer Festival medals and 2 World Beer Cup wins. The Imperial Red is the most-decorated beer, followed by the Double White. One of their most interesting brews is the Brett IPA, which is aged in chardonnay barrels with an addition of *Brett*. The downtown location hosts a guided tour every Tuesday, and both locations feature live music on a regular basis. If learning is more your style, sign up for a yoga class, or a beer/food pairing class. The brewery is dog and kid friendly. Daily food trucks (sometimes two) visit, and once you've had your fill of killer food and killer brews, fill your growler before you head home. **Downtown: 111 Marble Ave. NW, Albuquerque; Westside: 5740 Night Whisper Rd. NW, Albuquerque I Marblebrewery.com**

BOSQUE BREWING COMPANY: In addition to the main brewery in Albuquerque (the San Mateo tap room), they operate the Public House in the same city, and a satellite tap room in Las Cruces, with a new location coming in Bernalillo. They've taken home some hardware from both the World Beer Cup and Great American Beer Festival for their IPAs. Upscale bar food, burgers, and sandwiches are served on site, and their beers are available on a year-round and rotating basis. For something strong, try the Scotia Scotch Ale, and for something fruity, the Elephants on Parade has additions of raspberry, cranberry, and cherry. When in season, the Acequia fresh hop IPA is legendary. **San Mateo: 8900 San Mateo Blvd. NE, Ste. I, Albuquerque; Public House: 106 Girard Blvd. SE, Ste. B, Albuquerque; Las Cruces Tap room: 901 E. University Ave., Bldg. 985, Ste. B, Las Cruces I bosquebrewing.com**

CANTEEN BREWHOUSE: Formerly known as Il Vicino Brewery, the Canteen Brewhouse has taken multiple prestigious awards from all over the world, including Great American Beer Festival, North American Beer Awards, and World Beer Cup to name a few. They pour five beers, including a German Pilsner, American wheat, American brown ale, IPA, and a stout. The food menu includes mostly sandwiches, but you can also order up soups, salads, and apps. Live music is often on the events calendar, and growlers are available to go. Kids and dogs welcome! **2381 Aztec NE, Albuquerque I canteenbrewhouse.com**

B2B BISTRONOMY: Burgers and beers are what you'll find (a lot of) here. They're a nanobrewery and a beer bar, so come thirsty! Their claim to fame is their emphasis on flavors, so you'll find fruits, barrel-aged brews, and of course, peppers. We recommend the Coconut Porter, Cherry Stout, and Oak Aged IPA, but for something a little off the beaten path, try the Pepper Saison. Also on tap are 34 beers brewed right in New Mexico, rounding out an incredibly diverse list of offerings. Growler fills are available, as are flights.

3118 Central Ave. SE, Albuquerque | bistronomyb2b.com

BACK ALLEY DRAFT HOUSE: Beer is the focus at Back Alley, where frequent tap takeovers, beer tastings, and cask events are the norm. Twenty-eight taps pour a rotating lineup of local, domestic, and import brews, and did we mention they also brew a few of their own? The New York Pizza Dept. is right behind them, and guests can order from their menu. Watch some sports on TV, play some darts, and be sure to get your growler filled before you head out.

215 Central Ave. NW, Albuquerque | facebook.com/Back-Alley-Draft-House

JUBILATION FINE WINES & SPIRITS: When you're ready to settle in for a quiet night, this is the place to go for a six-pack or specialty bottle—it was voted Best Beer Selection in Albuquerque, after all. Commit to a six-pack of one brew, or get in on a "make your own" package. And if you're in the mood for whiskey and wine, there's plenty of that to go around, too. **3512 Lomas Blvd. NE, Albuquerque | jubilationwines.com**

BOXING BEAR BREWING CO.: New Mexico's new schoolers aren't afraid to take some chances, even with very traditional styles. Their Body Czech Pilsner is crisp and refreshing in the New Mexico heat, and the Uppercut IPA is yet another example of how progressive and on-point the state's brewers are when it comes to using hops. The panini menu is food if you need it, but this isn't a place you go to eat. Thankfully, the beer alone is more than enough reason to visit. **10200 Corrales Rd., Albuquerque | boxingbearbrewing.com**

CHAMA RIVER BREWING: Grab a seat at the bar, order one of their medal-winning beers (they have 4 Great American Beer Festival golds and 4 World Beer Cup silvers to their name), choose a Southwestern-tinged entrée from their full restaurant menu, and revel in all that is New Mexico beer. **4939 Pan American Fwy., Albuquerque | chamariverbrewery.com**

DRAFT STATION ALBUQUERQUE: From the same team behind Chama River and Blue Corn Brewery, Draft Station gets by with a little help from their friends. Every tap is New Mexico beer, from their own breweries as well as other top spots such as La Cumbre, Bosque, and Marble. And the comfortable and modern tap room feels like a cool spot to down a few pints. **1720 Central Ave. SW, Albuquerque | draft-station.com**

SANTA FE

SECOND STREET BREWERY: Beer geeks, rejoice! When you head down to any of the Second Street locations, you can talk beer with a certified cicerone—all the serving staff are certified. And if that isn't convincing enough, they've taken home 2 Great American Beer Festival medals—one for the Rod's Steam Bitter and the other for Second Street Stout. You can also find some gluten-free options. They serve a fairly diverse menu that's reasonably priced, and if you're in the mood for something other than booze they've got you covered. Sit inside or out on the patio at both locations and listen to live music most nights each week. Both locations are family friendly (but leave

Fido at home)—the original location is more of a "locals" hangout, and the Railyard is in a trendier area. Growler fills are available at both locations. **Original: 1814 2nd St., Santa Fe; Railyard: 1607 Paseo de Peralta, Santa Fe | secondstreetbrewery.com**

SANTA FE BREWING CO.: Two Santa Fe locations and one in Albuquerque make up the Santa Fe Brewing Co. They serve up 8 year-round flagships, 3 seasonals, 2 barrel-aged sours, and 3 experimental brews. Three of their brews have medaled at Great American Beer Festival and 3 at the World Beer Cup. Grab a growler or six-pack to go at either of their locations. The original brewery and tasting room is where all the magic happens; it has a barrel cellar and a tasting room, along with food trucks. For more of a tap room feel, head over to the El Dorado Taphouse, and settle in with a few pints, wine, beer, or hard cider, and catch a game on TV. If you're in the Albuquerque area, the tap room is at the Green Jeans Farmery and offers 27 taps, wine, and hard cider. **Brewery: 35 Fire Pl., Santa Fe; El Dorado Taphouse: 7 Calienete Rd., Santa Fe; Albuquerque Tap room: 3600 Cutler NE, Albuquerque | santafebrewing.com**

THE COWGIRL HALL OF FAME: This is a beer and history lover's paradise, with beer and cowgirl history galore. Twenty-four beers, mostly from the western United States, are on tap, with a smaller variety of bottles. Not sure what to get? Order a flight. A full-service food menu is also available, and multiple network TV shows and publications have given the food high marks. Almost as strong as their devotion to cowgirls is their devotion to music. Live shows are scheduled every night of the week. Giddy-up! **319 S. Guadalupe St., Santa Fe | cowgirlsantafe.com**

BLUE CORN BREWERY: From the same folks behind Chama River Brewery in Albuquerque, Blue Corn Brewery in Santa Fe might feel like nothing more than a small scale local brewery, but their 2 gold and 3 silver Great American Beer Festival medals (plus 3 World Beer Cup medals) suggest that they might be up to something more interesting. Order a pint of the oatmeal stout—it's outstanding—and an entrée from their New Mexican menu (because you're here and why order the same old pub fare you can get anywhere?). You'll thank us. You can also visit their downtown cafe where they feature casual New Mexican cuisine, pub fare and their award-winning, beer. **Brewery: 4056 Cerrillos Rd., Santa Fe/ Café: 133 Water St., Santa Fe | bluecorncafe.com**

FIRE & HOPS: For a cozy gastropub experience that offers carefully selected craft beers on tap and in bottles, this is the place to go. Many of the craft beers on hand are from New Mexico, with a healthy offering from other Western states, the East Coast, and across the world. Frequent beer-focused events are on their schedule. An outdoor covered patio is dog-friendly and has a lovely hops garden. While beer is the focus, wine and cider are also available by the bottle and glass. Food consists of some unique twists on old favorites and some truly unique dishes on small and large plates. **222 N. Guadalupe, Santa Fe | fireandhopsgastropub.com**

DRAFT STATION SANTA FE: This surprisingly large spot on Santa Fe Plaza offers an outdoor roof deck overlooking the plaza in addition to a large indoor space with everything from dimly lit tables to a bright and open room with ping-pong tables. Choose your own adventure, order from the predominantly New Mexico-driven tap list (can't go wrong with Bosque or La Cumbre), and soak up the beauty of Santa Fe. **60 E. San Francisco St., Santa Fe |**

draft-station.com

JOSEPH'S OF SANTA FE: Do yourself a favor and book a table at Joseph's next time you're in Santa Fe. The beer list is tight but powerful (we enjoyed a La Cumbre Elevated IPA with our meal), but the food... easily one of our top three meals of the year. The restaurant interior feels like Santa Fe—funky, eclectic, and authentic—and the food is local, fresh, artfully designed, impeccably prepared, and beautifully presented. Share a few plates as the sun goes down for an experience that will cement your love of Santa Fe. **428 Agua Fria St., Santa Fe | josephsofsantafe.com**

TAOS

ESKE'S BREW PUB & EATERY: You can't spend time in New Mexico without trying at least one chile beer, so you'd better make it Eske's Great American Beer Festival award-winning Taos Green Chile Beer, made with New Mexico chiles. Six of their own beers are on draft, some year-round and some seasonals, and they also have 3 guest taps and a few New Mexico brewers' in cans. Pull up a seat in their homey adobe building and sip some beers, eat some fab Mexican food and burgers, and settle in for a game of ping-pong in the backyard. Live music acts perform on the outdoor patio area, where you can sit around the band in an intimate setting while they perform. **106 Des Georges Ln., Taos | eskesbrewpub.com**

TAOS MESA BREWING: Live music is a mainstay at this venue, with two large outdoor stages that overlook the Sangre de Cristo Mountains and one indoor stage. Hang out in the tap room and try their year-round beers or special/seasonals on tap, then head outdoors for a ping-pong or cornhole tournament. Food on the menu is mostly tacos, and you can also snag a burger or their famous Frito pie. Kids and dogs are welcome, and when you're ready to head out, grab a growler of your favorite brew to go. **20 ABC Mesa Rd., El Prado | taosmesabrewing.com**

ANGELFIRE

ENCHANTED CIRCLE BREWING: Newly opened in early 2016, Enchanted Circle's beer program is led by Head Brewer Kyle Yonan who made the jump up to the mountains from Blue Corn Brewery in Santa Fe. Yonan's recipes are tried and true to the styles he brews, but he stretches out with his yearly wild hops brew, where a team of volunteer pickers forages wild hops from the New Mexico countryside that Yonan turns into a unique beer full of local terroir. **20 Sage Ln., Angel Fire | facebook.com/Enchanted-Circle-Brewing-155087768180589**

IDAHO

The great wide open of Idaho is perfect for getting in touch with your inner spirit of adventure. Many of its breweries pay tribute to that spirit with envelope-pushing brews, while others focus on tradition and leave the high-adventure feats up to you. Either way, no matter what you've experienced before pulling up a seat for some fine Idaho brew, you'll no doubt be coming back for more.

BEST SPOTS FOR OLD SCHOOL BEER STYLES

Payette Brewing shucks the trends and focuses on brewing only the best-tasting beers, while Selkirk Abbey Brewing Company's beers are traditional Belgian-style through and through.

BEST SPOTS FOR NEW SCHOOL BEER STYLES

10 Barrel Brewing is home to the Crush Cucumber Sour and some high ABV/high IBU IPAs that push the limits of hops flavor, and Barbarian Brewing brews up some risk-taking beers with a thriving sour and mixed-fermentation program.

BEST SPOTS TO ENJOY A MEAL WITH YOUR BEER

Bittercreek Alehouse has some thoughtful upscale food selections and a 39-tap draft lineup; Bar Gernika's chorizo and croquetas are not to be missed, and neither is their international bottle list.

MOST STYLISH TAPROOMS AND BARS

10 Barrel rocks the Old World industrial architecture like no other while Selkirk Abbey Brewing Company looks more like a monastery than a brewery inside and has the beers to match.

MOST AWARD-WINNING BREWERY

Grand Teton Brewing Company has swept up a half dozen medals from the Great American Beer Festival as well as another 4 from the World Beer Cup.

BEST UNIQUE BEER EXPERIENCE

Mad Bomber Brewing Company was founded by U.S. Army veterans, and the military-themed decor pays tribute to that background. The homey interior has an inviting fireplace to gather around, too!

BOISE

BITTERCREEK ALEHOUSE: (right) With 39 options on draft, a completely stacked cellar, and a thoughtful menu that includes the likes of duck confit poutine and käsespätzle, they check all the boxes and then some. An attentive staff is on hand to answer questions about food and menu choices and make recommendations on beers, and the tap list is updated on the website daily. Some nights live music plays indoors, creating a cozy setting between musicians and patrons. Order up a flight and take home a growler of your favorite. **246 N. 8th St., Boise | bcrfl.com/bittercreek**

10 BARREL BREWING CO. PUB: The main brewery is in Bend, Oregon, but if you're in the Boise area, you're in luck. The corner pub rocks some Old World industrial architecture and allows pub-goers to sit indoors or out. The food is pub fare, with burgers, pizza, and other treats. An impressive selection of beers on tap rotates regularly. The Apocalypse IPA is a flagship IPA with 6.8 percent ABV and 70 IBUs, and the S1NISTOR Black Ale is a schwarzbier with a touch of chocolate and a smooth finish. For something a little out of the ordinary, the Cucumber Crush Berliner Weisse is a tart concoction that's super refreshing. Kids and dogs are welcome.

830 W. Bannock St., Boise | 10barrel.com

CLOUD 9 BREWERY: A balance of source and craft is the basis of Cloud 9's beers and food menu. Beer is merged into the food menu as much as possible, and they've put a rather large emphasis on finding Idaho-sourced and organic ingredients when possible. Patrons who want something that's not beer can select from their nanobrewed root beer, ginger beer, and birch beer. One of their flagships is the Salted Caramel Stout, which is a smooth dark ale that's served only on nitro. The NSN (Never Say Never) IPA is at the lower end of hops-bomby IPAs with 45 IBUs, but if a hops-bomb is what you're looking for, definitely order the Fallen DIPA, which clocks in at a whopping 115 IBUs. Tours are offered, and if you're in the mood for a growler, you can grab one of theirs or one from the guest taps. **1750 W. State St., Boise | cloud9brewery.com**

PAYETTE BREWING COMPANY: Named after the famed Trapper Francois Payette, the brewery is all about its Idaho roots and the spirit of adventure. Their beers are less trend-based and more about creativity and what tastes good. We like their Blood Orange Rustler, which is an IPA high on sweet blood-orange flavor, that packs a hoppy punch. The Mutton Buster is a brown ale that's full of flavor, earthy, and nutty, with a kick of cocoa and malt. And the North Fork Lager is a sessionable lager that's perfect for cooling off after a day of hiking and rafting. Live music and events are frequently at the tap room, and you can take a crowler or growler to go. **733 S. Pioneer St., Boise | payettebrewing.com**

BAR GERNIKA: This is a tiny "hole-in-the-wall" Basque district pub with 8 rotating taps serving regional beers such as Fort George 3-Way, Stone En-joy By, Green Flash Sea to Sea Lager. Their impressive bottle list includes local craft brewers as well as micro domestics and imports—and some really outstanding Belgian imports! For a snack, the croquetas are out of this world, and nobody should leave without trying any of their chorizo dishes. **202 S. Capitol Blvd., Boise | bargernika.com**

BREWER'S HAVEN: They offer a massive selection of craft, local, and import bottles and cans, and 6 rotating taps at each store. Plus all the homebrew equipment you will need to start you own batch. Check the website's events calendar for tastings and special events. Food can be ordered in, and sometimes food trucks visit. Growlers can be filled, too. On the first Saturday of the month homebrew classes are offered (make a reservation). Dogs and kids are welcome! **1795 S. Vista Ave., Boise / 1311 12th Ave. Rd., Nampa | brewershaven.com**

BOISE BREWING: It's hard to miss Boise Brewing while driving by—the bold graphic exterior proudly screams there's beer inside—and that boisterous attitude extends to the warehouse-style interior within. It's big, open, semi-industrial, slightly raw, but generally energetic with live music a few times a week. The beer itself is good—solid renditions of familiar styles plus fun and flavorful one-offs—and their community-supported brewing membership program is a cool way to engage with the community. **521 W. Broad St., Boise | boisebrewing.com**

BARBARIAN BREWING: They're a bit more civilized than the name suggests, but these Boise brewers aren't afraid to push local palates with sour and mixed-fermentation beers. The tap room is small with standard-issue reclaimed wood accents, but the risk-taking beers are worth seeking out. **5270 W. Chinden Blvd., Garden City | barbarianbrewing.com**

WOODLAND EMPIRE ALE CRAFT: A perfect example of how quality ingredients and proximity to them impacts beer, Woodland Empire's flagship IPA, City of Trees, is on paper nothing particularly special—no Citra hops, no sexy Southern-Hemisphere hops—just Chinook, Centennial, and Cascade. But the quality of the ingredients and their deftness in using them transforms them into something special and pulls out the soft tropical notes that care and well-timed picking can impart. The tap room's shabby chic aesthetic is fairly de rigeur among craft breweries today, but it's light, pleasant, and a fine place to enjoy the range of beers they brew—from malty ambers and barleywines to nicely hopped IPAs and fruity and floral Belgian-style saisons, tripels, and quads. **1114 W. Front St., Boise | woodlandempire.com**

THE PANHANDLE

CRAFTED TAP HOUSE + KITCHEN: Where else can you go for 50 taps, a gastropub menu, and turtle races? Crafted Tap House has everything from local brews to international, and because the entire bar staff has gone through formal cicerone training, making a good selection should be a snap. The food menu is pure indulgence, with comfort foods such as chicken and waffles and huge burgers and sandwiches, and if that's not enough, you can top things off with a fried Oreo. And don't forget that you can take a growler to go. Live music, tap takeovers, and turtle races round out their events schedule, and the venue is family friendly. **523 Sherman Ave., Coeur d'Alene | craftedtaphouse.com**

SLATE CREEK BREWING COMPANY: It's all about the company you keep at Slate Creek, where conversation replaces a room full of TVs, and the locals store their mugs on the wall. Some of the year-round offerings include the Norse Nectar Juniper Pale, the 6 Weight IPA, and the Harper's Oatmeal Stout. Three seasonals and 2 guest beers are also on tap, and you can grab a growler to go. The only food served on site is peanuts, but you can either order in or come on a night when one of the visiting food trucks is on premises. **1710 N. 4th St., Ste. 115, Coeur d'Alene | facebook.com/SlateCreekBrewingCo**

MAD BOMBER BREWING COMPANY: The founders are U.S. Army veterans, and the cozy tap room pays homage to that background in its military-themed decor. Two of their beers, Fatman IPA and St. Nicholas Pale Ale, were named after two of the founding members killed in the war, and 50 percent of the sales from these two beers is donated to the Wounded Warrior Project. Other noteworthy beers include the Crossfire IPA, Carbon Stout, Claymore Double IPA, and Silver Land Double IPA. There's no food on site so you'll want to come with a full stomach (or your own food), or you can order from the café next door. Dogs are invited to the tap room, where they can hang out while you play games with friends. And as if that's not enough, the brewery was voted Best Local Brewery of 2015 by *The North Idaho Business Journal*. **9265 N. Government Wy., Hayden | facebook.com/Mad-Bomber-Brewing-Company**

LAUGHING DOG BREWING: Outdoor enthusiasts and dog lovers alike will appreciate the "fetchingly good beers" served in Laughing Dog's tasting room near Schweitzer Mountain. Warm up with the Dogfather Imperial Stout or Alpha Dog Imperial IPA, or try the brewery's Purebred single-hopped American Pale Ale series. Take home one of their signature growlers filled with one of 15 beers on tap. Their Test Kitchen serves breads, salads, and soup. Dogs are invited to join in on the fun, too! **1109 Fontaine Dr., Ponderay | laughingdogbrewing.com**

SELKIRK ABBEY BREWING COMPANY: The brewery is Belgian to its core, with an monastery-like decor, and, of course, Belgian beer. Four year-round offerings include Belgian-style beers: Chapel, Infidel, Deacon, and Guilt. Infidel is a spicy Belgian IPA with a bit of sweetness to balance the hops. They have a nice lineup of other Belgian-inspired seasonals, too. On tap at the tasting room you'll find 7 of their own brews, as well as 4 guest taps. Food carts are frequent, and sometimes live music graces the tap room. **6180 E. Seltice Wy., Ste. 102, Post Falls | selkirkabbey.com**

IDAHO

POST FALLS BREWING COMPANY: They brew good beer and look good doing it at Post Falls Brewing. One step inside might have you thinking you're in Seattle or Portland rather than the edge of Washington and Idaho—the industrial warehouse vibe and modern branding would be more at home in an urban center. Style wise, it's hard to pin them down, but you can't go wrong with their hoppy offerings. **112 N. Spokane St., Post Falls | postfallsbrewing.com**

SOUTHEAST IDAHO

GRAND TETON BREWING COMPANY: The views and the brews are equally spectacular in this southeast Idaho brewery. And you'll know you're in a good place when you walk in and see their trophy wall, which includes a silver from Great American Beer Festival for their super sessionable Ale 208. Other noteworthy beers include the Sweetgrass APA, Bitch Creek ESB, and the Howling Wolf Weisse Bier. For the sour lovers, they have a gose, Berliner Weisse, a *Brett* saison (rated 96 by *Craft Beer & Brewing Magazine®*) and other barrel-aged delights. And if something sweet and non-alcoholic is more your style, they have a lineup of kettle-brewed sodas. Outside is a rather large grass area to sprawl out and relax, play games, or chill with some food from the visiting food truck. **430 Old Jackson Hwy., Victor | grandtetonbrewing.com**

IDAHO BREWING COMPANY: Known for their traditional styles, Idaho Brewing is a down-home, no frills tap room filled with malt-forward beers that evoke comfort and warmth. Try the Highland Scotch Ale or the Wolf's Oatmeal Stout, and feel the warm waves of beer nostalgia wash over you. **775 S. Capital Ave., Idaho Falls | idahobrewing.com**

UTAH

The state's restrictive approach to beer—no draft may be served over 4.0 percent ABV, packaged beer over 4.0 percent ABV must be sold through state liquor stores or poured from bottles at breweries and restaurants, etc.—has put up numerous roadblocks for would-be brewers. But an intrepid few have braved the maze of government regulation, and that determination and drive have produced some very, very good beer.

UTAH

BEST SPOTS FOR OLD SCHOOL BEER STYLES

While Wasatch isn't purely an old-school brewer (they're happy to plan in new-school styles as well), they're particularly good at tasteful and elegant renditions of classics.

BEST SPOTS FOR NEW SCHOOL BEER STYLES

EPIC's (right below) beer lineup appears to grow by the day, and it seems like they're always packaging yet another new brew whether it's Sour Brainless on Peaches or a saison brewed with wild sage or one of the best pumpkin porters we've tasted.

BEST SPOTS TO ENJOY A MEAL WITH YOUR BEER

The Bayou's (right above) Cajun and Creole-inspired menu pairs deliciously well with the vast array of beer they offer in bottles (and the few they're allowed to sell on draft).

MOST STYLISH TAPROOMS AND BARS

We made our first visit to Squatters' brewpub more than 20 years ago, and when we look at it now we're struck by just how many breweries have followed in the same footsteps of raw and revived industrial buildings as breweries and brewpubs.

MOST AWARD-WINNING BREWERIES

Redrock, Wasatch, Uinta, and Squatters have all notched double-digit tallies of GABF medals over the years … no small feat.

BEST UNIQUE BEER EXPERIENCE

Zion Canyon Brewing sits under the cliff spires of Zion National Park, one of the most inspiring locations we've ever seen for a brewery… plus it's only a short walk from the park's southern campgrounds.

SALT LAKE CITY

UTAH

THE BAYOU: Winner of a host of "best of" awards, The Bayou is a beervana with a Cajun- and Creole-inspired menu full of unexpected items. Its 27 taps pour 4.0 percent ABV or less beer, and a stellar bottle collection (4.0 percent ABV and higher) boasts more than 300 choices (we were really tempted to buy that bottle of Pelican Mother of All Storms barleywine on our last visit). Only those 21+ are invited to the venue, however, so leave the younglings at home. **645 S. State St., Salt Lake City | utahbayou.com**

EPIC BREWING COMPANY: Four of EPIC's brews have gone home with a Great American Beer Festival medal: Utah Sage Saison, Brainless on Peaches, Imperial IPA, and 825 State Stout. And that's not including the dozens of other trophies they've scored in other competitions. We've fallen hard for two of their beers, Big Bad Baptist and Double Skull Dopplebock, both of which scored a near-perfect 99 from the CB&B discriminating judges. Be warned before you visit that the tap room only seats a handful of people (it is literally one of the smallest tap rooms we've ever seen in any brewery of any size, but of the 6 seats available, two of them are ADA compliant), and if you want to drink on site you'll have to order an entrée from the full kitchen (thanks to Utah liquor laws!). All the trouble is worth it, though. They have a massive beer fridge with an outstanding selection of their beers in bottles and cans you can take home. For the full-on experience, try the EPIC Brewing Sugarhouse Pub, where a full menu and full lineup of full-strength beers (in bottles, of course, because this is Utah) are available. **Brewery: 825 S. State St., Salt Lake City; Sugarhouse Pub: 1048 E. 2100 S., Ste., 110, Salt Lake City | epicbrewing.com**

SQUATTERS CRAFT BEERS: It's not just the Great American Beer Festival and the World Beer Cup who have fallen in love with Squatters beers (multiple—*multiple*—times), we rated their Hoppy Pils a 94 in 2016. Other notable brews include Outer Darkness RIS, Fifth Element, and 529 Oud Bruin. Catching them fresh is becoming easier, with tap rooms expanding to Salt Lake, Park City, and the Salt Lake International Airport. Burgers, comfort food, and pizza have a big presence on the food menu, and when they can, they buy local and organic. Lots of musical and beer-themed events are on the calendar, so you'll want to plan ahead. Go home with a six-pack of bottles or a growler. **147 W. Broadway, Salt Lake City | squatters.com**

UINTA BREWING COMPANY: There's no shortage of variety in Uinta's 23 beers on tap—they've got something for just about anybody. Their King's Peak (right) has nabbed six Great American Beer Festival medals, Cutthroat Pale Ale (right) has won four, Sum'r has won two, and Schwarzherz, Baba, and Bristlecone have each taken home one. That's not to mention the 9 World Beer Cup trophies they've gone home with! They have a thriving barrel program and are debuting 2 gluten-free beers soon. You'll find a full-service menu and can take a tour, watch TV, or just chill for a few hours while you're there. Kids and dogs are definitely welcome! **1722 S. Fremont Dr., Salt Lake City | uintabrewing.com**

AVENUES PROPER: This is the first brewery in Utah allowed to sell its own beer *and* beer from other breweries on tap and in bottles, and it has a pretty remarkable menu. Local brews, domestics, and an import or two can be ordered. We recommend Proper's own Foreign Gentleman Stout and their Avenues Annual Saison. Lunch, dinner, and brunch are available, with comfort foods being the central theme. **376 E, 8th Ave., Ste. C, Salt Lake City | avenuesproper.com**

RED ROCK BREWING COMPANY: Art and creativity shine in the creations brewed here. Their Draft Classes are 4 percent ABV or lower (Utah law). The Fine Line beers aren't tied to Utah's restrictions, and some on this line top off at over 10 percent ABV. Their experimental line is Artist Palette, where tradition meets uniqueness. The Paardebloem is a Belgian-style ale that uses dandelion as a bittering agent, and it won the gold at the Great American Beer Festival in Experimental beer, and was featured in a New Belgium collaboration for the Lips of Faith series. Their Organic Zwickelbier won a silver at Great American Beer Festival. On the food menu is brick-oven pizza, sandwiches, and comfort food. You can buy a bottle or growler to go. **254 S. 200 W., Salt Lake City | redrockbrewing.com**

BOHEMIAN BREWERY: The interior feels like a cozy ski lodge with its huge stone fireplace and wood beams, and you can walk out to the outdoor patio to take in some of the incredible mountain views. They've got a collection of vintage Vespas upstairs, as well as taxidermy mounts and paintings. But let's talk beer. They stick to the *Reinheitsgebot* (German purity law), brew in small batches, and because they specialize in lagers, they take longer to ferment. The food menu is best described as "Old World meets pub fare" and is made from all-natural ingredients. When you leave, you can pick up a twelve-pack of cans or a growler to go! **94 E. 7200 S., Midvale | bohemianbrewery.com**

2 ROW BREWING: Their tagline is "little brewery, huge flavor," and 2 Row delivers with new-school recipes and tight execution. Because of the restrictive draft laws in Utah (which do not allow draft beer over 4 percent ABV), all of their beer is bottled, so sampling at the source requires visiting their bottle shop (don't call it a tap room). And because it's all bottled, they're a bit more restricted in the variety of "bottle shop exclusives" and the like that you'd normally expect at a brewery. Nonetheless, they've pressed forward with aggressively hopped beers such as their flagship Accelerator IPA and earthy and funky farmhouse beers such as Dangereux saison, and are creating a buzz in the beehive state. **6856 S. 300 W., Midvale | 2rowbrewing.com**

ꞋDEN & PARK CITY

ꞋAN BREWING COMPANY: After the head brewmaster retired ꞋꞋꞋer in the U.S. Air Force, the long-time homebrewer indulged ꞋꞋꞋ for beer and started a brewery. Their beers range 4–10 ꞋꞋꞋthere's quite a variety to be found here. We recommend ꞋꞋꞋ with 65 IBUs and a piney, floral, grapefruit character, ꞋꞋꞋnAle Blood Orange Honey Wheat. Take a tour, then sit down in the tasting room for a flight of samples. Bottles are available for sale, as are growlers. **1258 Gibson Ave., Ogden | talismanbrewingco.com**

WASATCH BREW PUB: We're apparently big fans of Wasatch—their Last One In scored a 90, Devastator a 92, and Snap Down a 95 from our super selective blind-tasting panel. And Great American Beer Festival, World Beer Cup, and North American Beer Awards have also deemed them pretty worthy. The food menu is full of burgers, sandwiches, pizza, and some other comfort-food favorites. If you're not into the beer (just pretend for now, okay?) you can order from the liquor and cocktail menu. Growlers, bottles, and cans are available to go. **250 Main St., Park City | www.wasatchbeers.com**

SLACKWATER PIZZERIA: We couldn't be more excited about craft brewers' renewed focus on flavorful low-ABV beers, and Slackwater Pizzeria has likewise embraced the trend (partly out of necessity and partly by choice). Their draft list spans a flavorful range from light and tart gose to a punchy rye stout, and if those don't excite you, they have another 60 or so varieties in bottles that surely will. Fun and creative pizza makes for a perfect beer accompaniment. **1895 Washington Blvd., Ogden | slackwaterpizzeria.com**

ZION NATIONAL PARK

ZION CANYON BREWING COMPANY: Southern Utah's first microbrewery can be found at the base of Zion National Park. So when you're tapped out after a day of hiking the park, you can grab a nice cold one before you head back to your campsite. We recommend the Conviction Stout, which is a dark, roasty, chocolaty stout, and the Red Altar, which is a malty, citrusy American red. While you're sipping and recharging enough to get back to base camp, you might catch a live music act or karaoke, and you can grab a bit of pub fare either inside or on their gorgeous outdoor patio. Growler fills are poured on site, which means that once you're motivated enough to head out, you can grab some brew for a nightcap. **2400 Zion Park Blvd., Springdale | zionbrewery.com**

MOAB

MOAB BREWERY: They've garnered the attention (and awards, of course!) of Great American Beer Festival, World Beer Cup, North American Beer Awards, and other national beer contests, and have the hall of fame in the tap room to prove it. We like their Dead Horse Ale and Desert Select Scotch Ale, but they have a pretty healthy list of great beers to choose from. If cold beer isn't enough to beat the desert heat, they have a massive selection of house-made gelatos. The family-friendly brewery also has a food menu of pub fare, salads, and hand helds, among other offerings. Cans, bottles, and growlers are all available to go. **686 S. Main St., Moab | themoabbrewery.com**

ARIZONA

Arizona is a state of extremes, from the deserts of the southern part of the state to the mountains around Flagstaff, and the state's brewers exhibit a similar type of range. From wild spontaneous fermentations to thoughtful and historical accurate stylistic renditions, the brewers of Arizona have accomplished it all.

BEST SPOTS FOR OLD SCHOOL BEER STYLES

This honor goes to Historic Brewing Company because history isn't just a part of their name; it defines their approach to brewing their wide variety of classic styles.

BEST SPOTS FOR NEW SCHOOL BEER STYLES

Arizona Wilderness takes this category by a landslide with their wild spontaneous coolship beers, their foraged-ingredient beers, and their tame-only-by-comparison mixed-culture and kettle-soured beers.

BEST SPOTS TO ENJOY A MEAL WITH YOUR BEER

McFate Brewing's ultra modern brewpub and tap room offer creative pub fare in a well-designed space that you won't want to leave.

MOST STYLISH TAPROOMS AND BARS

You might not feel cool enough to drink a beer inside Tap and Bottle in Tucson, but don't worry—we all feel that way after stepping into this beautifully designed beer space... so get over it, and order a pint already.

MOST AWARD-WINNING BREWERIES

Four Peaks won their first GABF medal in 1998 and won their most recent one in 2013... no wonder they were such a hot acquisition target for AB InBev.

BEST UNIQUE BEER EXPERIENCE

If you love creative beer and want to see what the vanguard of brewers is doing at the very bleeding edge of experimentation, you absolutely must visit the Arizona Wilderness brewpub.

PHOENIX

ARIZONA WILDERNESS BREWING CO: Arizona Wilderness opened in 2013, and just a few months after opening, RateBeer named them the best new brewery in the world. The imaginative beers highlighting unique ingredients sourced from local farms and from the wilderness itself have been lauded. They've done 70 or 80 beers that center on foraged or local ingredients—including everything from the relatively staid (such as dates and lemongrass) to the rather obscure (smoked pine cones, Anderson wolfberry, and creosote flowers). Almost all of the beer made at Arizona Wilderness is sold at the pub, and the ever-changing tap lineup is driven by what in-season ingredients they can source. You can always expect something different each time you visit. Mixed-culture beers supplement the steady stream of kettle-soured brews that are popular in the pub, such as Bear Wallow—a dry-hopped Berliner Wiesse. **721 N. Arizona Ave., Gilbert | azwbeer.com**

WREN HOUSE BREWING COMPANY: This cozy neighborhood brewery is inside a house built in 1922 and is a pretty mixture of rustic and industrial. They've created some truly artistic brews, using ingredients such as elderflower, ginger, chiles, chai, and currant, to name a few. Our recommendations begin with Jomax, an oatmeal stout that they've experimented with a few times to create KitKat Jomax and Whiskey Barrel Vanilla Double Jomax. Also of note are Wren House IPA and Black Caddis. Trivia nights and food trucks are a mainstay, and don't forget to grab a growler before you head out. **2125 N. 24th St., Phoenix | wrenhousebrewing.com**

SCOTTSDALE

MCFATE BREWING COMPANY: Small batches are McFate's forte, and because of their specialty, they rotate beers often. Expect to see some of the more traditional beers, along with experimental brews, seasonals, and casks that are only available at the brewpub. Most of the beers are available for growler fills, and they offer cans from other breweries for sale as well. Beers we recommend include American Pale Ale, Candy Bar Milk Stout, Double Oatmeal IPA, Cuppa Jose Milk Porter, and El Ultimo Mexican Hot Chocolate. Pub snacks, salads, and wood-fired pizzas are all on the menu. If you're looking for a little wellness with your beer, there's a weekly yoga class. Live music and tasting events can also be found. **7337 E. Shea Blvd., #105, Scottsdale / 1312 N. Scottsdale Rd., Scottsdale | fatebrewing.com**

PAPAGO BREWING CO.: Papago is a full-service brewpub that serves 30 beers on tap, more than 500 in bottles, and brews its own, too. Beers on hand include craft domestics and imports. Of their own list, we recommend the Elsie's Milk Stout (and its sister Elsie's Irish Coffee Milk Stout), Coconut Joe, Coconut Coffee Stout, and Hop Dog IPA. For food they serve up gourmet hand-pressed pizzas with draft beer baked into the crust, salads, and hand helds. **Papago Plaza Shopping Center, 7107 E. McDowell Rd., Scottsdale | papagobrewing.com**

TWO BROTHERS TAPHOUSE AND BREWERY: Artisan beer and food are what Two Brothers is all about. Rotating beers are brewed and served on site, and they feature a diverse list of year-round, seasonal, and special release beers. Some of the favorites include the Ebel's Weiss, Wobble IPA, and Sidekick Extra Pale Ale. If something with a little more kick is your style, beer cocktails are also on the menu! The food menu includes some traditional American favorites. **4321 N. Scottsdale Rd., Scottsdale | twobrothersbrewing.com/restaurants/scottsdale-tap-house-and-brewery**

TEMPE & CHANDLER

FOUR PEAKS BREWING CO.: Eight brews started Four Peaks, and they're the mainstays to this day. Seasonals and cask ales also make their way onto the taps, so there's always something new when you visit. Their most popular beer (by far) is the Kilt Lifter, a traditional Scottish strong ale with a note of smokiness. Also noteworthy are the Vanilla Porter, Barrel-Aged Cherry Porter, and Sirius Lifter. Food includes burgers, sandwiches, and pizza. To take a tour of the brewery, there's a charge of $10, which includes two tasters. **1340 E. 8th St., #104, Tempe | fourpeaks.com**

TOPS LIQUORS & TASTE OF TOPS: Spend an evening here and you'll have no shortage of beers to choose from, with 30 rotating taps and 600 bottles/cans. And if you find something on tap that you really like, you can get it in a growler to go. The majority of the beers come from the Western United States, but imports from Belgium and Italy also make up the list. Hosting a party? They have a gigantic list of kegs you can get from them, too! No kitchen is on site, but you can order in food or grab some takeout from a nearby restaurant. **403 W. University Dr., Tempe | topsliquors.com/tasteoftops**

HUSS BREWING COMPANY: This is a neighborhood hangout that has 20 revolving taps that come from other craft brewers, as well as their own lineup of beers brewed on site. Five of the year-round beers can be found all the time, and also come in cans—some of the most popular are the Scottsdale Blonde, Koffee Kölsch, and That'll Do IPA. Three seasonals are usually on tap, and the most recent noteworthy concoction is the Rice Pudding Porter. Flights are served on the coolest looking chalkboard lazy suzans, and once you've found your favorite beer, take it in a growler to go! **1520 W. Mineral Rd., Tempe | hussbrewing.com**

SANTAN BREWING: SanTan has been brewing craft beer for the greater Phoenix area since 2007, and lately they've taken their act on the road, expanding distribution of their cans into greater Arizona and California. Expect expertly prepared pub food from the kitchen, a clean and comfortable (but not stuffy or sterile) warehouse-style interior, and a full lineup of their core and seasonal beers, including Mr. Pineapple pale wheat, and Sex Panther porter. **8 S. San Marcos Pl., Chandler | santanbrewing.com**

TUCSON

1912 BREWING COMPANY: Bring the family to this homey brewery, where the kids can play on the train table while the parents relax and enjoy a pint. Or take it outdoors and get a game of cornhole on. Eight beers are on tap, as well as 4 wines, cider, and mead. Bottled beer is also available. The most popular brew is their Cerezo Cherry Gose, which is a collaboration with the Ermanos Craft Beer & Wine Bar and Borderlands Brewing Company, and it's made with yogurt *Lactobacillus* culture and Oregon cherry puree. Food trucks and local bands are frequent visitors, but they also serve up artisan popcorn. **2045 Forbes Blvd., #105, Tuscon | 1912brewing.com**

BARRIO BREWING COMPANY: A trip to this revitalized industrial warehouse brewery is perfect for getting out of the heat with its 12 beers on tap, selection of bottles from other brewers, and a full bar. Some recommendations we'd make include the Barrio Blonde, Barrio Blanco, and Barrio Rojo—this Scottish ale won bronze at the Great American Beer Festival. For something super strong try the Barrio Imperial Stout, and for a fruitier hoppier quaff, go for the Rae's Ruby Red IPA. A full-service kitchen can whip up a burger or a panini, or some wicked-good Mexican fare. **800 E. 16th St., Tuscon | barriobrewing.co**

TAP & BOTTLE: Quite possibly the coolest spot to buy and drink craft beer in Tucson, Tap and Bottle is a hipster dreamland of Edison bulbs, chalkboards, and live-edge wooden communal tables. But style aside, what really makes it great is a superbly curated draft list and extensive bottle menu (for on site consumption and to-go) with a strong focus on top-tier national breweries (and some very good locals thrown in for good measure). **403 N. 6th Ave., Tuscon | thetapandbottle.com**

DRAGOON BREWING COMPANY: This brewery is nestled in an industrial park and might be a little hard to find, but once you're there you've hit gold. The beers are on point, and the Dragoon IPA and Stronghold Session Ale (their two year-round offerings) are their most sought-after. Locally grown wheat is used to brew the Ojo Blanco and Half Moon, and New Mexico blue corn is used in the Saison Blue. We also recommend trying the Lazarus, which is a special release barleywine, and Cinco, a Russian Imperial stout. Food comes in the form of food trucks, but they're cool with you ordering in from other places, too. The crowd is predominantly of the hipster variety, and in our experience the staff was attentive and knowledgeable. You can take a growler or crowler to go, too! **1859 W. Grant Rd., #111, Tucson | dragoonbrewing.com**

1702 PIZZA & BEER / THE ADDRESS BREWING CO.: On our first visit to 1702, a number of years ago, we couldn't help but chuckle at the cooler next to the taps that read "Your Colorado Beer Headquarters." We had flown in from Colorado and were searching for local and unique beer, only to find that cooler and its intention to take us back. Thankfully, we ordered some pizza (delicious) and a few non-Colorado drafts (also delicious), and enjoyed the Tucson beer experience. Today, that cooler is gone, but the rotating list of 46 imports and domestic micros are still there on tap, and their bottle list is now much too large to fit in that single cooler. They've even added a nanobrewery to the location to brew their own beer. The menu is full of gourmet pizzas and calzones, but if you don't see something you like (and you'll be hard-pressed not to!), try the build-your-own option. **1702 E. Speedway Blvd., Tucson | 1702az.com**

YUMA

PRISON HILL BREWING COMPANY: This is the only craft brewery within a 165-mile radius, and it's named for the iconic Territorial Prison nearby. Four of its own beers are on tap, and we recommend the Melon Felon IPA, which is a light, hoppy beer with a big dose of melon flavor that comes from one of the brew's experimental hops. Its Sally Porter is a chocolaty, coffee-flavored dark brew that's rounded out with notes of cinnamon and amaretto. On the gastropub side, some very intriguing concoctions are coming out of the kitchen, including fried avocado, poutine, and a smoked meat plate to name a few. **278 S. Main St., Yuma | prisonhillbrewing.com**

DESERT EAGLE BREWING COMPANY: This downtown Mesa brewery with a biker-bar vibe has a lineup of 12 beers on tap, and there's something for every palate. The Red Mountain Ale has a toasted nut flavor and a nice dose of hops rounds out the finish. The Buzz Bomb IPA is light, crisp, and refreshing, with a nice hoppy finish. The taps rotate on a regular basis, and throw in some seasonals and special releases at times, too. On the events calendar are near-nightly themed events such as happy hour, open mic, and live music—Sundays are the build-your-own-bloody beer bar. The kitchen serves up some great pub fare. **150 W. Main St., Mesa | deserteaglebrewing.com**

THE BEER RESEARCH INSTITUTE: Mesa's first brewpub has a rotating lineup, with a focus on Belgian-style ales and aggressive West Coast–style ales. Our recommendations include Lolli, an Imperial Belgian blonde with an 8.2 percent ABV; Morning Sex, a sweet coffee stout brewed with cold-press coffee from a nearby coffee purveyor; Dark Side Till I Die; and Love Goes

Sour. Fifteen beers are usually on tap, and most are on the high-ish side of the ABV scale. Food on the menu is mostly Mexican and is divided into "Tacos" and "Not-Tacos." But for a real treat, order up the Meat Candy, which is—you guessed it—candied bacon. **1641 S. Stapley Dr., Mesa | thebeerresearchinstitute.com**

FLAGSTAFF

DARK SKY BREWING CO: Take a break in this rather large tasting room, which has the coziness of a mountain lodge and the coolness of a neighborhood hangout. While they promise to have at least 6 beers on tap at a time, we found 18, many of which were Belgian-inspired or IPAs—but what you find on tap will depend on the season. They use a special process to make their beers gluten-reduced. Some favorites include Hot Chocolate, a Serrano pepper stout; Lemon Drop Belgian Saison; and Bear Jaw Imperial Cherry Brown. They also brew batches of gluten-free beer on a separate system. Live music and visiting artists can be found in the tasting room, and don't forget to grab a crowler or growler to go! **117 N. Beaver St., Flagstaff | darkskybrewing.com**

MOTHER ROAD BREWING CO.: Grab a beer and hang out in the tasting room and play board games—or better yet, the outdoor patio with a fire pit, where you can kick back with your dog. The brewery's name is an homage to John Steinbeck's callout of Route 66 in the *Grapes of Wrath*. All right, so what can you expect for beer? For the most part, IPAs of various styles, a brown ale, and a Kölsch. We recommend Lost Highway, which is an imperial black IPA with notes of bitter orange chocolate, orange zest, and roasted malts. The Tower Station American IPA has aromas of pineapple and tangerine, with hops flavors of grapefruit peel and pine. And Gold Road is a Kölsch that's got a biscuit malt body, with hints of pear and apple. Food is provided by Pizzicletta next door, which has created a menu just for the tap room. Growlers are available for most beers. **7 S. Mikes Pike St., Flagstaff | motherroadbeer.com**

HISTORIC BREWING COMPANY: Four flagship brews are the backbone of Historic's beer lineup, rounded out by seasonals, barrel-aged beers, and some experimental brews, too. The Piehole Porter is a pie-lover's chocolaty, fruity dream, starting with a brown porter, with cherries and vanilla beans. The Opposable IPA is an English IPA big on grassy, piney, citrusy flavors, and the Joy Rye'd Rye Pale Ale includes spicy malts and is dry hopped with three hops. About 8 beers are on tap in the tasting room, half of which are rotating taps. Food trucks are sometimes on site. This is a dog-friendly brewery so you can hang out and play some outdoor games with your best friend, too! **4366 E. Huntington Dr., Flagstaff | historicbrewingcompany.com**

PEORIA

FREAK'N BREWING COMPANY: Spend an afternoon in the small, inviting tasting room, where you can sample the 8 beers on tap and enjoy a bite from a food truck (or bring your own). Some standouts include the Sweet Thang Crème Brulee Imperial Milk Stout, Raspberry Wheat brewed with raspberry puree, and American Hero Pale Ale. Sometimes live music plays in the tasting room, and growlers are available to go. **9299 W. Olive Ave., #513, Peoria | freaknbrew.com**

NEVADA

Nevada was a desert for craft beer for a long time, but the last decade has seen multiple oases spring up throughout the state as creative brewers embrace the pioneering spirit of the West. With breweries offering everything from Old World mixed-fermentation sours to classic English-style ales and more trendy hoppy beers, it's easier than ever to hit the craft-beer jackpot.

BEST SPOTS FOR OLD SCHOOL BEER STYLES

We're not sure whether Brasserie St. James fits in the old school category due to their focus on traditional Belgian-style farmhouse and wild beers, or new school because they're on the front end of American breweries embracing these styles. Either way, they should be on your radar.

BEST SPOTS FOR NEW SCHOOL BEER STYLES

Likewise, IMBiB could fit into new or old school with their focus on everything from fruited Berliner Weisse beers to barrel-aged *Brett* saisons. And for hopheads, they brew great IPAs as well.

BEST SPOTS TO ENJOY A MEAL WITH YOUR BEER

James Beard award-winning chef Todd English's P.U.B. wins hands-down here. It just might be the best upscale gastropub fare you've ever had.

MOST STYLISH TAPROOMS AND BARS

Tenaya Creek Brewery offers great beer in a clean and modern space with floor to ceiling glass showcasing the brewhouse.

MOST AWARD-WINNING BREWERIES

Great Basin and Chicago Brewing share top medal honors, with Big Dog nipping at their heels.

BEST UNIQUE BEER EXPERIENCE

Let's be honest here—every brewery and beer bar in Nevada offers gambling of some sort, and it's a weird and wild experience to grab a pint of fantastic and freshly brewed beer while playing hands of video poker.

LAS VEGAS

TODD ENGLISH P.U.B.: Todd English P.U.B. was the first, and is still one of the best, places on the strip to drink excellent craft beer. With more than 50 taps and a James Beard Award-winning chef on staff, it will make you feel as if you've hit the jackpot amid the sea of macrobrew-only bars throughout town. And in true Vegas style, the menu is packed full of just about everything the mind can imagine—brunch, raw bar, upscale entrees, pub fare, burgers, steaks…and that's just scratching the surface. In between beers, the Bloody Mary is a meal in and of itself, topped off with a shrimp cocktail, deli cuts, veggies, and a slider. **3720 Las Vegas Blvd. S., Las Vegas I toddenglishpub.com**

BANGER BREWING: We couldn't pass up the chance to give a shout out to a place that offers a $30 wristband for all you can drink all day. This Fremont Street brewery offers up 10 of their own beers on tap, and we recommend their caramel coffee-flavored Morning Joe Kölsch, the 84-IBU-strong Hop Bang Boom American IPA, and the El Heffe Jalapeno Wheat hefe. But what's a Vegas venue without its food menu? Straight-up pub fare is on deck, along with their build-your-own fry menu—top those suckers with just about anything you can imagine putting on them. Tours are available almost every day of the week by reservation, and when you're all set, you can grab a growler to share (or not) back at the hotel. **450 Fremont St., #135, Las Vegas I bangerbrewing.com**

CHICAGO BREWING COMPANY: Off the strip is a slice of Chicago, and this cozy brewpub serves up its own select list of Great American Beer Festival–winning beers, as well as a decent selection of domestic and import craft-beers—we especially appreciate their devotion to Trappist ales! The All Nighter blonde is a floral, nutty, hoppy ale that's taken home 3 GABF medals, and the Weizenheimer is a German-style wheat with hints of banana and clove that's hazy and super carbonated, and it's taken home gold from GABF. Breakfast is served 24 hours a day, and you can also grab a steak, burger, or pizza for lunch or dinner. Growlers are available to go, too! **2201 S. Fort Apache Rd., Las Vegas I chicagobrewinglv.com**

GOOSE ISLAND PUB: The Hard Rock Hotel & Casino might be an unlikely spot for a beer bar, but mid-2016 saw the opening of the first ever Goose Island pub outside out of Chicago right there. The tap list includes your Goose faves (and some of our favorites, such as their Sofie farmhouse ale), but the bottle list is where it goes full Vegas. All the "sisters" are there—Gillian (farmhouse ale with strawberries), Juliet (wild ale with blackberries), Halia (farmhouse ale with peaches), Madame Rose (Flanders-style oud bruin), and Lolita (wild ale with raspberries)—and if you really want to show your friends how big a high roller you are, drop $100 on a bottle of Bourbon County Brand Rare stout and live the good life. **4455 Paradise Rd., Las Vegas I hardrockhotel.com/las-vegas-restaurants/goose_island_pub**

BIG DOG'S BREWING COMPANY: It's all about the dogs at this off-the-strip brewery, which has 15 of their own beers on tap and 19 guest taps from all of the Western U.S. and beyond. The Red Hydrant Brown took home a gold at the 2006 and 2010 World Beer Cup, and is a 2012 Great American Beer Festival silver medalist. You might also try the Dirty Dog

IPA, or the Peace Love & Hoppiness American pale ale. The Draft House side of things has a neighborhood brewpub vibe but also has a casino, and it serves up Midwestern cuisine. The Front Porch is a smoke-free dog-friendly patio where you can sip, eat, watch a live show, and play with your (furry) best friend.

4543 N. Rancho Dr., Las Vegas | bigdogsbrews.com

TENAYA CREEK BREWERY: In their new, expanded location, Tenaya Creek is brewing up 6 year-round brews, and a rotation of 8 seasonals. Their old-meets-new industrial-styled tap room is separated from the brewery with floor-to-ceiling glass walls, so you can watch the action while you're enjoying what's on tap. The Bonanza Brown is an English-style brown that's won bronze at the Great American Beer Festival, and we also recommend the Imperial Stout, Hefeweizen, and Hop Ride IPA. Food trucks are on hand a lot of the time, and if you need to stretch out after hours hunched over a slot machine, yoga classes are on the schedule at times, too! **831 W. Bonanza Rd., Las Vegas | tenayacreek.com**

ACES & ALES: This is, hands down, the most unique beer bar we've ever been into. On our last visit to the Nellis location, we were initially taken aback at the absence of windows in the place, and the interior would feel dark and pubby if it weren't for the glow of video poker games at *every* bar seat. The other thing we noticed was the cigarette smoke—yes, that apparently is still legal in Nevada. Our bartender was animated and personable, but the real fun began when perusing the glass-front coolers full of vintage bottles. Prices are high, even by Vegas standards, but if you're on a winning streak, why not drop a Ben Franklin on a bottle of 2013 Firestone Walker Parabola and celebrate? You don't even have to gamble to get lucky sometimes—we saw Drie Fonteinen Oude Gueuze on the menu and ordered a bottle only to find that it was a 4-year-old vintage that wasn't marked up as such. Win! **East Side: 3740 S. Nellis Blvd., Las Vegas / West Side: 2801 N. Tenaya Ave., Las Vegas | acesandales.com**

HENDERSON

LOVELADY BREWING: The tap room of this super-cozy, rustic/industrial brewery has many tables and bar-top seating throughout. A fancy shuffleboard game is located on one side of the room, and cornhole is also on deck. Although there's no kitchen, you can buy some snacks, bring your own, or wait for one of the food trucks to arrive on select days. On the patio, you can let the kids and leashed dogs play while you kick back and relax. We recommend the 9th Island, which is a pineapple kettle sour, the HopAtomic imperial IPA, and the Café Femenino, a coffee-spiked porter. For their weekly "super spectacular keg," one keg of a tweaked version of one of their regular beers goes on tap. Past examples include Angry Red Headed Hawaiian, which was half 9th Island and half Love Triangle (red ale) with jalapeños, and Girl Scout Cookie Beer, which was their Porter with coconut, cocoa nibs, and Caramel Delite cookies. **20 S. Water St., Henderson | loveladybrewing.com**

BAD BEAT BREWING: To escape the gaming and get into a smoke-free/vape-free environment while sipping some of the best beers in Henderson, head over to Bad Beat. Some of their most popular beers include the Hoppy Times IPA, the Gutshot Irish stout, and Bluffing Isn't Weisse, a hefeweizen. They have a thriving barrel program, and their Morning Payoff is an American imperial stout aged in Nevada 150 bourbon barrels with an addition of coffee at the end of the aging process. As far as food goes, you can bring your own, order some for delivery, or grab some from the food truck. **7380 Eastgate Rd., #110, Henderson | badbeatbrewing.com**

CRAFTHAUS BREWERY: True to its name, CraftHaus is brewing up batches that are true to tradition, but also creative twists on traditional beers, and some that we'd call a touch whimsical. The mid-century modern tap room is bright and open, with enough color and metal furniture to make any 1950s-style-lover giddy. For some of the traditional brews, try the Resinate IPA and Evocation, a Belgian-style saison, or Comrade, a Russian imperial stout aged in Las Vegas Distillery's whiskey oak barrels. Now for the whimsical. Evocation comes in a version that's "tweaked with Chilean wine must," and their seasonal Glitter Bomb is a sour table beer with glitter in it (we're not even kidding). Brewery tours are on Saturdays and cost $10, which also includes a 4-glass tasting flight. **7350 Eastgate Rd., #110, Henderson | crafthausbrewery.com**

RENO & SPARKS

BRASSERIE SAINT JAMES: There's a lot to love about the historic, old-world brasserie-style brewery and restaurant—they've swept up many Great American Beer Festival, North American Beer Awards, U.S. Open Beer Championship (and more!) medals, and we rated their Daily Wages saison at a 95. A few of their award winners include Third Man, a Belgian triple; Red Headed Stranger, a farmhouse ale; and the aforementioned Daily Wages. They have a brunch and dinner menu that serves creatively crafted rich food that's to-die-for, and seating can be found indoors, outdoors, and on the roof. Wine and cocktails are also on the menu. Some nights feature live music and happy hour. Take a growler to go, too! **901 S. Center St., Reno | brasseriesaintjames.com**

THE BREWER'S CABINET: Things might be done on a small scale at this small-batch nanobrewpub, but that's exactly what frees them from limitations of fads and other industry limitations. And despite their size, they have 15 beers on tap. You might try the Dirty Wookie, Tahoe Amber Ale, Tahoe Beer, and Apparition Double IPA, or the Roaster's Imperial Coffee Stout, Twenty One. A small kitchen onsite offers a lunch and dinner menu with foods that pair nicely with the beers—it's a hearty selection of salads, sandwiches, burgers, and steaks. Cans, growlers, and kegs are available to go. **475 S. Arlington Ave., Reno | thebrewerscabinet.com**

IMBiB CUSTOM BREWS: With their specialty being Old World–barrel-aged beers, it should come as no surprise that most of their offerings are Berliner Weisses, saisons, and other Belgian-inspired brews. They also have a malt-forward lineup with cream ales, bocks, and stouts to name a few. Their Oatmeal Stout and Red Rye IPA are two of their most popular malt-forward beers, and Cherry Berliner Weisse and their Barrel Aged Belgian Red are their most sought-after sours. No onsite kitchen means you either need to order in or wait for a food truck, but every now and again they host ticketed beer/food-tasting events. **785 E. 2nd St., Reno | imbibreno.com**

RENO PUBLIC HOUSE: A relative newcomer to the Reno beer scene, this subway-tiled quasi-industrial spot hits the hipster high notes, but their beer program is fantastic and it's more than worth a visit. Draft lines balance with about 50 percent going to breweries in the region, another 30 percent going to top picks from the United States, and the remaining taps dedicated to smart and savvy German and Belgian selections. **33 St. Lawrence Ave., Reno | renopublichouse.com**

PIGEON HEAD BREWERY: Lagers are the specialty at Pigeon Head, but that's not all they brew—a small selection of seasonals and an IPA can also be found on the tap list. Among the most popular are Red Rye Lager, Black Lager, IPL, and Pilsner, and some of their past not-lagers included Toasted Coconut, Graham Cracker, Black Wheat Wine with French Oak, and Jalapeno IPA. Food trucks are on site, or you can order in. Crowlers and growlers are available to go. **840 E. 5th St., Reno | pigeonheadbrewery.com**

SILVER PEAK RESTAURANT & BREWERY: Silver Peak is the lovechild of a Culinary Institute–trained chef and business-man-turned-college-educated brewer. Both locations serve up 6 of their regular house brews and a handful of seasonals, and the River Peak location also has other brewers on tap. Most notable are their Silver Peak IPA, Red Roadster, and Peavine Porter, but some of their noteworthy seasonals include the Raspberry Berliner Weisse and the Lupi Double IPA. Lunch and dinner are at both locations, and we recommend the pizzas—the dough is made with spent grains from the brewery. **Silver Peak: 124 Wonder St. / River Peak 135 N. Sierra St., Reno | silverpeakbrewery.com**

UNDER THE ROSE BREWING COMPANY: This is a neighborhood brewery through and through, with a super-casual (and fun!) tasting room. Play bocce ball, foosball, or ping-pong to your heart's content while you sample some of their amazing beers. Most of the beers are Belgian-inspired, but you can also order up an APA, IPA, or porter, to name a few. Eleven taps include a list of regular beers and seasonals. Food trucks are on site frequently, and it's a kid- and dog-friendly venue.

559 E. 4th St., Reno | undertherosebrewing.com

GREAT BASIN BREWING CO.: Nevada's oldest brewery started more than 20 years ago, and even after the bank said nobody would want to drink the beer, they persevered. Today, they have 14 rotating taps, 2 tap rooms with full kitchens, and they make fresh bread daily with spent grains. The Reno location is also a concert venue. Now let's talk beer. They've won 14 Great American Beer Festival medals and 7 at World Beer Cup. We recommend their 385 Scytale, the 404 Scytale, Ich Bin Ein Berliner, Dark Side Vanilla Stout, and the Bourbon Barrel-Aged Icky 2016. Now for the food. A lot of it incorporates their own beers, and you'll find some traditional American fare alongside some interesting twists on old classics. Kids are welcome, but better be sure to leave the dog at home.

846 Victorian Ave., Sparks | greatbasinbrewingco.com

ALIBI ALE WORKS: On the north shore of Lake Tahoe lives Alibi Ale Works, a brewery focused on a balance between traditional European styles and hops-forward American styles…and a few experimentals here and there, too. Their 3 core beers include Porter, Saison, and Pale Ale, and innovative one-offs occasionally make their way onto the taps. Food trucks visit frequently, and so do live bands. The brewery is a 21+ establishment so be sure to leave the younglings at home, but well-behaved leashed dogs are welcome in their place. **204 E. Enterprise St., Incline Village | alibialeworks.com**

TONOPAH

TONOPAH BREWING CO.: The brewhouse inside Tonopah is an incredible custom-designed schematic from Bavaria that's heated by steam and run by pneumatic controls. Because of their devotion to tradition, the system allows for decoction and step infusion. We recommend the Mucker Irish Red, a malty beer with a full body that's dry hopped with whole leaf hops. The families who own the brewery also own two wineries, and their wines are available by the glass or bottle. The kitchen serves up barbecue, and you can enjoy your orders inside or outside on the patio.

315 S. Main St., Tonopah | tonopahbrewing.com)

WASHINGTON

Home to more acres of hops than anywhere else in the world, Washington is of key importance to craft beer in more ways than one. The state's brewers have taken that proximity to top quality ingredients to heart, brewing boundary-pushing renditions of IPAs and double IPAs, and more recently delving into the sour and wild side of brewing.

BEST SPOTS FOR OLD SCHOOL BEER STYLES

Our top two spots for this category aren't too far from each other in Bellingham—try Chuckanut if well-brewed lagers are your thing, and if your tastes swing more to the English side, then Boundary Bay is stocked with classic renditions of a number of styles.

BEST SPOTS FOR NEW SCHOOL BEER STYLES

There are almost too many to list: Fremont, Holy Mountain, Cloud-burst, Wander, Structures, and 3 Magnets are all pushing the enve-lope with hops, mixed fermentation, and barrel aging.

BEST SPOTS TO ENJOY A MEAL WITH YOUR BEER

Brouwer's Cafe is a one-of-a-kind vintage beer and Belgian food experience that is an absolute must for any fan of Belgian beer. On our last visit, we drank a 2003 bottle of Cantillon Lou Pepe Kriek and asked ourselves, "Where else can you do this in the United States?"

MOST STYLISH TAPROOMS AND BARS

We'll give the nod to Aslan Brewery on the strength of their very cool yet comfortable modern tap room, but the custom bar table cut in the shape of Rueben's Brews "r" logo (right) is a pretty fantastic detail.

MOST AWARD-WINNING BREWERIES

Big Time, Elysian, Pyramid, Chuckanut, Boundary Bay, and Silver City all have Great American Beer Festival medal counts in the double digits.

BEST UNIQUE BEER EXPERIENCE

Sitting in the Bale Breaker tap room or on the patio, surrounded on three sides by their family's hops fields, drinking one of their hoppy beers with some of the best hops to come out of those fields... it doesn't get much better than that.

SEATTLE

Navigating this beautiful Pacific Northwest city can be geographically tricky, due to the clean bisection Lake Washington provides to the Seattle Metro area. Just two bridges, one of those being a toll road, offer the only means of crossing the giant lake that lives right in the center of the area.

The up-and-over method of getting around the lake will take you far north of the city, and going around it on the other end will take you far south. Both options also offer a smattering of fantastic breweries, a bit of a cultural apology for the inconvenience. The abundance of beer, brewers, and hops in this area leaves you no shortage of haunts to hit, regardless of the region of Seattle you've landed in.

BALLARD/FREEMONT

The Ballard/Freemont section of Seattle boasts the most breweries and beer bars per square mile in the state. Most of the destinations are within walking distance of each other, but you may need more than one day to hit them all. If you choose just one area of Seattle to visit, this will most likely be your best bet.

FREMONT BREWING COMPANY: They're one of the fastest growing breweries in the state, and have become a favorite of locals, constantly packed to the rafters with patrons. Fremont is well-known for its innovative and delicious combinations poured through the two Randalls that are in frequent rotation. Hang out in their Urban Beer Garden, where you can either order in or bring your own food, and leave with a growler, keg, bottle, or can of your favorite brew. **1050 N. 34th St., Seattle | fremontbrewing.com**

BROUWER'S CAFÉ: (right) This is a must-visit for beer fans. With 64 taps, an extraordinary 300-bottle list (their philosophy is to rely on the brewer regarding whether a beer is cellar-worthy and how long it can age), an extraordinary selection of whisk(e)ys, Belgian-inspired cuisine, and a full schedule of beer events, this is a destination for local (and visiting) craft-beer fans. **400 N. 35th St., Seattle | brouwerscafe.com**

REUBEN'S BREWS: Reuben's is a brewery so well loved by Seattle beer fans that they brewed the official beer for the 2016 Seattle Beer Week. With a Randall program just as impressive as Fremont's, as well as several Great American Beer Festival awards under its brewing belt, Reuben's is a beer experience that you shouldn't miss. **5010 14th Ave. NW, Seattle | facebook.com/ReubensBrews**

STOUP BREWING: When biologist and cicerone Robyn Schumacher teamed up with her equally science-and-beer-obsessed friends Lara Zahaba and Brad Benson, the union formed one of the most impressive beer spots in Seattle. Equal parts flavor explosion and beer-science innovation, Stoup is a brewery to watch. Grab a pint and order up something to eat from their frequent food trucks, or order in for delivery. Love something you tried? Have it packaged in a growler to go. **1108 NW 52nd St., Seattle | stoupbrewing.com**

POPULUXE BREWING: With a tap room that's easy to get comfortable in, a regular rotation of food trucks on weekends, and a couple Washington Beer medals to its name, Populuxe is growing in popularity and is a

force to be reckoned with in the Ballard beer scene. They rotate their beers regularly and always try to have something malty, hoppy, dark, and light on tap at all times. In addition to indoor seating, an outside courtyard features picnic tables, fire pits, games, and room for the kids to run around. **826B NW 49th St., Seattle | populuxebrewing.com**

BOTTLEWORKS: Bottleworks has been selling great craft beer in Seattle since 1999, and their yearly anniversary beer releases (done in partnership with breweries such as New Belgium, The Bruery, Lost Abbey, Stone, and others) are legendary. With more than 950 different packaged beers, including many vintage and cellared options, there's always something fun to discover. **1710 N. 45th St., #3, Seattle | bottleworks.com**

CAPITOL HILL/DOWNTOWN/QUEEN ANNE

HOLY MOUNTAIN BREWING: Stop in for a pint at the current cool kid on the Seattle brewery block. Old World meets New on Holy Mountain's tap list, where the beer styles range from pale ale to mixed-fermentation saisons and barrel-aged farmhouse ales—beer styles that stand out among the IPAs and hoppy pale ales that Seattle is known for. They don't make any one beer year-round, and they don't have a flagship beer, so every visit to the brewery is an adventure. Some of their bottles are one-offs (so make sure to grab some while you're there), and some will be re-released. And when Holy Mountain decides to host a beer-pairing dinner, it sells out in minutes. **1421 Elliott Ave. W., Seattle | holymountainbrewing.com**

THE PIKE BREWING COMPANY: If you're the sort who wants to stop into Pike's Place Market and watch the professional fish throwers, then pop in next door for a pint and a bite to eat. Pike's has been serving beer to Seattle locals and tourists since the 1980s and has earned a soft spot in the craft-beer-loving hearts of Washingtonians ever since. They have a full calendar of events listed on their website. **1415 1st Ave., Seattle | pikebrewing.com**

THE PINE BOX: If you're brave enough to fight Seattle traffic, head over to The Pine Box, which was established by Ian Roberts, a cofounder of Seattle Beer Week and the former bar manager of Brouwer's Cafe. The Pine Box is housed in a former mortuary (hence the name) and pours a well-curated beer list from its 30 taps. The Pine Box also hosts beer events regularly, so keep an eye out. **1600 Melrose Ave., Seattle | pineboxbar.com**

CHUCK'S HOP SHOP: (Below) You can stock your beer fridge at one of the most well-trafficked and well-stocked bottle shops in town. With regular food trucks, a tap room featuring 41+ beers, and a crowd of beer geeks in attendance, Chuck's is more than your average bottle shop. Look for bottles you can't find anywhere else in the city, order a flight, and grab a bite at the food truck parked outside. **656 NW 85th St., Seattle and 2001 E. Union St., Seattle | chucks85th.com and chuckscd.com**

ELYSIAN BREWING: Of the four Elysian locations, the original Capitol Hill spot is still our favorite. Maybe it's nostalgia or maybe it's the big open warehouse feel, but it just feels like the perfect place to drink an Elysian beer. Fall is the best time to visit—Elysian is one of the best and most creative at pumpkin beers, and they could have as many as 8 different pumpkin beers on tap at any time. In addition, if you get a chance to try The Fix coffee imperial stout, don't pass that up—it's one of the best coffee stouts we've tasted. **1221 E. Pike St., Seattle | elysianbrewing.com/capitol-hill**

CLOUDBURST BREWING: Steve Luke, former experimental brewer for Elysian, struck out on his own and opened Cloudburst in early 2016. The tap room is about as roughly spartan and industrial as they come, but Luke has clearly spent much more time designing creative beers

than decorating the tap room. Speaking of the beers, Cloudburst seems unburdened by West Coast–style expectations, and their constantly evolving lineup of hazy, juicy IPAs bears more resemblance to New England than the PNW. Expect a handful on tap at any time, giving hopheads plenty of territory to explore. Farmhouse ale fans will enjoy their multiple iterations of saison, and there's usually a stout or two for dark-beer fans. If the bare bones tap room isn't your speed, look for their beers on tap at better beer bars around Seattle. **2116 Western Ave., Seattle | cloudburstbrew.com**

COLLINS PUB: Another downtown favorite of beer lovers, Collins offers a standard pub menu with a fantastic tap list and a strong Belgian-centric bottle list as well (think Oud Beersel Oude Gueuze, Russian River Supplication, etc). **526 2nd Ave., Seattle | collinspubseattle.com**

THE MASONRY: More wood-fired pizza spot than bar, The Masonry's beer program is cool and slightly weird … much more interesting than most. Drafts delve deep into the Shelton Brothers stable, with German standouts Kulmbacher, Freigeist, and The Monarchy plus local hipsters Holy Mountain. Bottles are even more awesome, with everything from Ale Apothecary to Jester King to Monkish to Struise in the cooler. **20 Roy St., Seattle | themasonryseattle.com**

STANDARD BREWING: They've come a long way in just a few years on the strength of an impressive lineup of hoppy beers. Grab a bench in the modern beer garden, start with a session IPA and work your way up to the Philistine triple IPA. If you need a palate cleanser, try the stouts—they're pretty good with those, too! **2504 S. Jackson St., Seattle | standardbrew.com**

STUMBLING MONK: Comfortable old-school beer bar with a small number of well chosen taps. It's more of a low-key hangout spot for board games and beers with friends than an intense beer experience, but sometimes that's just what we want. **1635 E. Olive Wy., Seattle | facebook.com/pages/Stumbling-Monk/124848827850590**

UNIVERSITY DISTRICT SEATTLE

THE BURGUNDIAN: From the folks behind Brouwers Café and Bottleworks, this University-area spot is stylish and cool with a delicious bar menu of gastro-tinged comfort food. The beer list is a bit more nationally focused than others in Seattle, offering a complement to the more locally focused bars. And if you're the type who loves whiskey as much as you love beer, this is the place for you—their list of bourbons and whiskeys is as impressive as their beer list. **2253 N. 56th St., Seattle | burgundianbar.com**

BIG TIME BREWERY & ALEHOUSE: If you're in the UW area, Big Time is known for very good beer and fairly average food, but the food counter is separate from the bar so it's pretty easy to choose your own adventure. Try the Coal Creek Porter or one of their several IPAs. **4133 University Wy. NE, Seattle | bigtimebrewery.com**

LATONA PUB: It's cozy and fills up fast on busier nights, but the food is delicious and reasonably priced while the draft list is small but potent and diverse, regularly featuring everything from dank PNW IPAs to imported Belgian lambic. **6423 Latona Ave. NE, Seattle | 3pubs.com/Latona.html**

SODO/GEORGETOWN

SoDo is how the locals say "South Downtown," and it's also home to more than a few great breweries.

TWO BEERS BREWING CO.: This is an ever-expanding brewery making waves in the SoDo beer scene since 2007. They pride themselves on using local ingredients and partnering with local businesses. Yes, there are more than just two beers, but their motto is "Life is just a little more honest after two beers." Can't argue with that. They share a tasting room with Seattle Cider Company and have a patio, games, and food trucks on certain nights. They are dog friendly, but to visit the tasting room, you must be 21+. **4700 Ohio Ave. S., Seattle | twobeersbrewery.com**

SEAPINE BREWING COMPANY: Attractively rustic industrial space, creative approach to beer styles—Seapine is right up our alley. The nautically inspired Sea Witch stout is exquisite in its drinkability, and the Positron IPA plays up that unfiltered New England–style fruitiness. It's stylish, well-executed, and fun. **2959 Utah Ave. S., Seattle | seapinebrewing.com**

GHOSTFISH BREWING COMPANY: We've tasted plenty of gluten-free beer, and Ghostfish is some of the best we've had the pleasure to drink. If your mental image of gluten-free beer is stuff made with sorghum and brown rice syrup, then you're in for a treat at Ghostfish—they use true gluten-free malts, no sorghum, and have set out to make beer that stands up to the best in craft, where you wouldn't know the beer is gluten-free from the taste alone. In addition to the beer, their gluten-free kitchen offers up an impressive menu of food so good you won't miss the gluten at all.
2942 1st Ave. S., Seattle | ghostfishbrewing.com

SCHOONER EXACT BREWING CO.: The clean and comfortable tap room conveys a modern and polished vibe in the otherwise industrial space. A tasty kitchen menu makes a meal a no-brainer while enjoying the beer. Try the Hopvine IPA or the Hamma Hamma DIPA. **3901 1st Ave. S., Seattle | schoonerexact.com**

MOLLUSK RESTAURANT & BREWERY: For a proper meal and a great pint, stop in for the best of both worlds. Mollusk rose from the ashes of Epic Ales, a favorite brewery around town that closed far too soon. Mollusk opened to a sigh of relief from the locals and offered the same fantastically weird beer that they'd gotten used to. Check out their Biru Sencha, a green tea lager, Squid Eyes, a Schwarzbier made with squid ink, or Rose Petal Red, an amber ale brewed with...well, rose petals. A full food menu is available, along with beers, wines, cider, and cocktails.
803 Dexter Ave. N, Seattle | molluskseattle.com

GEORGETOWN BREWING CO.: Head to this beloved brewery for a pint of Seattle's own Lucille IPA, a sentimental favorite of those who cut their craft-beer teeth in the Pacific Northwest. Georgetown doesn't bottle and the keg distribution is limited, but they do have growlers to go, so this may be your only chance to sample a true Seattle brew. **5200 Denver Ave. S., Seattle | georgetownbeer.com**

WEST SEATTLE

BEVERIDGE PLACE PUB: This classic-style pub's draft lineup is heavy on high-quality locals with some national and international hotshots thrown in for good measure. The interior feels historically eclectic, comfortable like a classic European pub and outfitted with couches as well as tables so you can choose just how casual you'd like to go. If you're looking for food, you won't find much here, but they're cool about it and you're welcome to bring in or order in your own. **6413 California Ave. SW, Seattle | beveridgeplacepub.com**

THE BEER JUNCTION: This bar and bottle shop offers extensive coolers and shelves full of great local, national, and international brands. The up-front bar and corridor of beer coolers is perfect for enjoying a beer or two while you shop, but if you're hunting down something in particular, check their website—new releases are updated there weekly. **4511 California Ave. SW, Seattle | thebeerjunction.com**

NORTHWEST SEATTLE

NAKED CITY BREWERY & TAPHOUSE: A neighborhood brewpub with a deep lineup of their own beers as well as a dozen guest beers, Naked City lets you have your cake and eat it too. Beer-centric fare from the kitchen is solid, the beer garden is a great spot to drink a beer when weather allows, and the screening room helps make it a center of local activity. Try The Big Lebrewski Russian Imperial Stout if they have it, and if not, Cry Me A River triple IPA. **8564 Greenwood Ave. N., Seattle | drink.nakedcity.beer**

ÜBER TAVERN: The bar and bottle shop is nothing fancy from the outside, and the interior design is only marginally better, but that's not what you care about now, is it? Sixteen taps of really great beer (barrel-aged stouts, sour beers, class-leading IPAs), a few hundred bottles including vintage selection, no food, but lots of love ... and an indoor fire pit. **7517 Aurora Ave. N., Seattle, | uberbier.com**

EASTSIDE AND NORTH SIDE: LAKE CITY/ REDMOND/BELLEVUE

While the west side of Lake Washington is best known for its beer scene, the other side of the lake is no slouch.

HELLBENT BREWING COMPANY: Traveling north of the city, and over the top of the lake, you'll find Hellbent. Founded by a collective powerhouse of Great American Beer Festival award winners, long-time bar managers, and beer geeks (Jack Guinn, Chris Giles, Randy Embernate, and Brian Young), this is a place that has a soul much older than its gorgeous, newly opened tap room. Especially on sunny days, the patio itself is worth the drive north. This 21+ establishment regularly hosts food trucks and a handful of events throughout the year. **13035 Lake City Wy. NE, Seattle | hellbentbrewingcompany.com**

BLACK RAVEN BREWING COMPANY: In Redmond, the locals will insist you stop at this brewery with rapid growth due to a catalog of consistently good beer, as well as a regular rotation of new and innovative brews. Try Coco Jones Coconut Porter, a 2010 World Beer Cup gold medal winner;

their Morrighan Nitro Stout, which scored a bronze medal in the 2012 North American Beer Awards; or Nothing But Flowers Session IPA, which took a silver medal in the 2013 Washington Beer Awards. Kick back with some grub from one of the visiting food trucks, and be sure to grab a growler to go before you leave. **14679 NE 95th St., Redmond |** **blackravenbrewing.com**

GEAUX BREWING: (Below) In Bellevue, check out this small hidden gem of a brewery. With everything from an impressively delicious summer ale to a smoked ghost chili porter, this is a place that will please even the pickiest of beer snobs. Make sure to take some of that beer home in a crowler— they will seal one for you right on the spot. Food trucks are on site a few nights a week. **12031 Northup Wy., #203, Bellevue | geauxbrewing.com**

WOODINVILLE

Just northeast of the top of the lake sits what locals think of as "Washington's Napa" With a huge supply of wineries, distilleries, and breweries, this is a booze lover's paradise.

TRIPLE HORN BREWING CO.: A rotating lineup of food trucks and 12 beers on tap will keep you topped off, and if you find something you really love you can take home a bottle (on select brews) or even a keg full.

19510 144th Ave. NE, #6, Woodinville | triplehornbrewing.com

B-SIDE BREWING: In the industrial district, along with the Des Voigne Cellars winery, lives this microbrewery that serves up craft brews alongside their Des Voigne Cellars wines. When the weather is nice, they roll up the doors so people can sit outside, and on certain nights of the week, they host a visiting food truck. Growlers and kegs are available to go.

14125 NE 189th St., Woodinville | dvcellars.com

DIRTY BUCKET BREWING CO.: They brew small hand-crafted batches and are always releasing new recipes. Check the website before you go to see what's new and currently on tap. They are dog and kid friendly, so be sure to bring them along! **19151 144th Ave. NE, Woodinville | dirtybucketbrewery.com**

THE COLLECTIVE ON TAP: This beer bar offers some delicious barbecue and a well-stocked tap list featuring primarily Pacific Northwest breweries, but you'll find a few Colorado and California beers on the list. Monday nights are brewer's night, featuring a new brewery every week and a Q&A with the brewer. They offer a full menu of apps, salads, sandwiches, and pizzas.

17802 134th Ave. NE, #6, Woodinville | collectiveontap.com

REDHOOK BREWERY & FORECASTERS PUBLIC HOUSE: There's no denying Redhook's place in the history of American craft beer, and the brewery in Woodinville is both a great place to celebrate that history and an enjoyable spot for a meal and tap room—exclusive brew. **14300 NE 145th St., Woodinville | redhook.com/breweries/woodinville-brewery**

ARLINGTON

SKOOKUM BREWERY: The pub menu is pretty standard, but this warehouse brewery offers TONS of indoor and outdoor space for beer drinking with a quaint bar. Try Amber's Hot Friend—a "West Coast" take on a hoppy amber ale. **17925 59th Ave. NE, Arlington | skookumbrewery.com**

BELLINGHAM

CHUCKANUT BREWERY & KITCHEN: You can get your IPA fix at any number of other breweries in Washington, but Chuckanut's focus on brewing award-winning lagers sets them apart. On a warm day, their Kölsch is hard to beat. And on cooler days, their Dunkel or Altbier hit the spot. The kitchen is similar to the beer—definitely not sexy or groundbreaking, just honest, thorough, and familiar in a way that doesn't demand an expert palate or excessive tasting notes to understand. **601 W. Holly St., Bellingham | chuckanutbreweryandkitchen.com**

BOUNDARY BAY BREWERY & BISTRO: They've been at it a long time—more than 20 years—yet the beer tastes as current as ever. Fourteen Great American Beer Festival medals and another 10 from the World Beer Cup are solid proof that the beer they're making is some of the best in the state (and country, for that matter). What's really impressive is the range of styles they brew well—you can order everything from an English ESB to an double IPA to a Scotch ale or stout, and rest assured that what you'll get is satisfying and world-class.
1107 Railroad Ave., Bellingham | bbaybrewery.com

KULSHAN BREWING CO.: Kulshan has the Bellingham lifestyle angle on lock, if their collaboration beer with local mountain-bike maker Transition Bikes named "Party in the Woods" IPA is any example. What could be more refreshing after a day of pinning it on the trails or on the slopes than a can of tasty IPA? Both the beer and the tap room are favorites of locals, crowding the patio when the weather allows. Skip the saison, stick with the hops or the stouts, and grab a six-pack of cans on your way out to lubricate your next adventure. **2238 James St., Bellingham | kulshanbrewery.com**

WANDER BREWING: Stouts, porters, sours, and Belgian-style ales are the name of the game at Wander—another welcome break from PNW hops overload. The open industrial warehouse offers a feeling of space with the brewhouse in full view, and the live edge wood furniture softens the industrial feel just a bit. Their Wild Warehouse barrel-aged farmhouse ale won Great American Beer Festival gold in their first appearance—do yourself a favor and try that, one of their Millie-series sours, or the Global Mutt porter. **1807 Dean Ave., Bellingham | wanderbrewing.com**

STRUCTURES BREWING: Beards? Check. Flannel? Check. Handworked wood interior? Check. Structures is a bit of a hipster highlight reel, but the beer is so good, we'll forgive the clichés. Their juicy, hazy New England–style IPAs offer a counterpoint to PNW-dub dank, and their equal love of mixed-fermentation farmhouse and sour beers is just as exciting. **1420 N. State St., Bellingham | structuresbrewing.com**

ASLAN BREWING: Gorgeous modern tap room, creative food, and really good beer—what's not to like? The Bravo 15 IPA is one of the more creative mainline packaged IPAs we've seen—a bit of a risk but a differentiator, for sure. On the food side, gotta love those roasted yam tacos—vegan, gluten-free, and delicious. **1330 N. Forest St., Bellingham | aslanbrewing.com**

THE LOCAL PUBLIC HOUSE: Solid food, great beer, and a comfortable space are the cornerstone to any good pub experience, and The Local delivers on all three. **1427 Railroad Ave., Bellingham | facebook.com/TheLocalPublicHouseBellingham**

MT. BAKER

NORTH FORK BREWERY: It's not every day you come across a pizzeria, a beer shrine, a wedding chapel, and a microbrewery all in one, especially after a day on the slopes. It's a destination for craft-beer lovers and powder hounds, where bettys and bros can carve fresh pre-nuptial powder in what's often thought of as the country's most iconic ski destination. The brewery is in the foothills of Mt. Baker, the home to the legendary Banked Slalom snowboard competition, first put on by the inventor of the snowboard, Tom Sims. Their pub has a lineup of beers, barleywines, sours, lagers, and pizza. **6186 Mt. Baker Hwy., Deming | northforkbrewery.com**

TACOMA

ENGINE HOUSE NO. 9: This beautiful vintage space is ideal for beer drinking, whether you're in the mood for their house brews or the guest taps (from some of the best craft brewers in the country) are more your speed. They take their pub grub seriously, with pizzas, huge sandwiches, and some of the best burgers around. **611 N. Pine St., Tacoma | ehouse9.com**

PARKWAY TAVERN: A homey spot for beer-drinking locals, Parkway offers cheap no-frills burgers and sandwiches, a stunning tap lineup, and typical bar games such as pool and shuffleboard. **313 N. I St., #1, Tacoma | parkwaytavern.com**

NARROWS BREWING CO.: The beers themselves are good, without being individually noteworthy, but the modern tap room and the amazing waterfront view from the tap room make it worth the visit. **9007 S. 19th St., Tacoma | narrowsbrewing.com**

PINT DEFIANCE: This bottle shop and tap room is stocked with great beer to go and on draft. It's clean, friendly, and fun. **2049 Mildred St. W., Tacoma | pintdefiance.com**

OLYMPIA

THREE MAGNETS BREWING CO.: Hazy IPA? Yes. *Brettanomyces*-fermented Grissette? Yes. Creative full pub menu? Yes. A must-visit for us when we're in the area? Yes. Any brewery with enough confidence to poke fun at themselves by referring to their own hazy IPA as a "smoothie" is alright in our book. **600 Franklin St. SE, #105, Olympia | threemagnetsbrewing.com**

TOP RUNG BREWING CO.: These firefighters homebrewed in their spare time and put together the funds to launch Top Rung while still continuing to work as firefighters—a dedication to service we love to see. The tap room is spacious and clean without a kitchen (so bring your own), and the beers are honest and hard-working with no need for gimmicks. **8343 Hogum Bay Ln. NE, Lacey | toprungbrewing.com**

WEST SOUND

SILVER CITY RESTAURANT & BREWERY: Great beer and great food make Silver City a must-visit when you're in the area. Their Ziggy Zoggy zwickelbier is a beautiful and refreshing summer beer; Fat Scotch has a couple Great American Beer Festival golds to its name; and the Old Scrooge barleywine is a must-try when in season. For a full meal, try the clean and contemporary restaurant, and for a strictly beer-centric experience, the tap room and brewery, with 17 taps, is the way to go. **2799 NW Myhre Rd., Silverdale | silvercitybrewery.com**

SOUND BREWERY: Belgians and IPAs are the draw at Sound—that they pull off both with panache is an impressive feat. Grab simple but tasty pizzas in the tasting room/restaurant, a pint of Humulo Nimbus IPA or Monk's Indiscretion tripel, and enjoy. **19815 Viking Ave. NW, Poulsbo | soundbrewery.com**

VALHÖLL BREWING: They don't take themselves as seriously as they take the beer at Vallhöll. The style lineup is typically diverse with a little bit of everything in the mix, but their smaller brew system (3.5 barrels) means there's usually something new on the tap list. **18970 3rd Ave. NE, Poulsbo | valhollbrewing.com**

PROPOLIS BREWING: Propolis brews some weird and wild herb-centric beers that are entirely different from most of their peers in the state. Starting from vaguely Belgian-style bases (saison, dubbel, quad), they've made the styles their own with unique blends of farmed and foraged herbs and spices. Try the Beltane Elderflower Saison and buy as many bottles as you can for your friends back home. **2457 Jefferson St., Port Townsend | propolisbrewing.com**

VANCOUVER

LOOWIT BREWING COMPANY: This small neighborhood brewery just north of the Columbia River might get overshadowed by better-known Portland breweries just to its south, but their satisfying hoppy beers have been keeping locals happy for years. **507 Columbia St., Vancouver | loowitbrewing.com**

HEATHEN BREWING: These risk-takers love their IPAs dank and sticky and aren't afraid to load as much Washington state hops as they can into every IPA batch. The Feral Public House offers a full menu of pub fare along with a big lineup of Heathen beers (plus a few guest beers), while the brewery tap room typically keeps about 20 of their beers on tap, allowing your palate as much promiscuity as you desire. **5612 NE 119th St., Vancouver | heathenbrewing.com**

COLUMBIA RIVER

EVERYBODY'S BREWING: Just over the river from Hood River, Oregon, this brewery in White Salmon features a patio with an amazing view of Mt. Hood. Beer-wise, they may be best-known for the dank double IPA they call "Hoppy AF," but whether you're into heaps of hops or oatmeal stout is more your speed, they make a beer style for everybody. **151 E. Jewett Blvd., White Salmon | everybodysbrewing.com**

YAKIMA VALLEY

BALE BREAKER BREWING COMPANY: They're everything you'd expect from a brewery located in the hops-growing capital of the world. Bale Breaker has only been around a couple of years, but their access to the best hops from their family's hops farm that surrounds them, including the freshest wet hops, makes every beer they brew with the letters "IPA" in it something worth trying. The tap room itself is well-designed, open, and modern, and the perfect place to taste gorgeous expressions of hops after driving through the hops fields themselves. **1801 Birchfield Rd., Yakima | balebreaker.com**

TEN PIN BREWING: Former pro baseball player BJ Garbe returned to his hometown of Moses Lake, Washington, and took over operations of his family's bowling alley. A homebrewer himself, he added a 3 bbl system to the bowling alley on a hunch that customers would like it, and response was so good they christened a new standalone brewhouse capable of producing 7,500 barrels per year in early 2016. Despite their location in Hopstown USA, their brewing focus is a bit more diverse, so don't be afraid to order a Black Eyed Katy imperial stout along with that Head Pin IPA.
1165 N. Stratford Rd., Moses Lake | tenpinbrewing.com

SPOKANE

NO-LI BREWHOUSE: The huge patio out back overlooking the river, with benches and fire pits and lights strung throughout, makes for a perfectly comfortable hangout spot while enjoying No-Li brews. The kitchen kicks out pub standards, while the brewhouse riffs across a broad range of styles, from IPA to stout and even some wild farmhouse ale experiments.
1003 E. Trent Ave., Spokane | nolibrewhouse.com

MANITO TAP HOUSE: Fifty taps and the full-on gastropub-style menu full of creative and well-made pub fare are what got us in the door, and the bottle list stocked with multi-year vintages of standout beers such as Fremont Bourbon Abominable, Deschutes Abyss, and Firestone Walker Stickee Monkey is what kept us there. The covered outdoor patio allows you to enjoy fresh air rain or shine, and the wood and metal interior manages to feel both industrial and human at the same time. This is a really cool spot, and a must for beer lovers when in Spokane. **Manito Shopping Center, 3011 S. Grand Blvd., Spokane | manitotaphouse.com**

BELLWETHER BREWING CO.: You'd expect a brewery out here in hops-growing country to focus on, well, hops. But Bellwether bucks convention and does their most creative work with a variety of other herbs instead. From braggots to gruits to herb-infused Hefeweizens, they offer flavorful off-kilter beers that make them more than just another me-too brewery. But if you absolutely must have an IPA, they have one of those, too. **2019 N. Monroe St., Spokane | bellwetherbrewing.net**

PINTS ALEHOUSE: The design itself isn't especially memorable, but they keep the lights low and keep the focus on the beer. And from a beer perspective, Pints doesn't disappoint. Roughly two dozen taps flow with an even mix of Washington State and national/international big names, and they regularly break out cellared and special kegs. **10111 N. Newport Hwy., Spokane | pintsalehouse.com**

PERRY STREET BREWING: One of the best-looking breweries in Spokane, Perry Street Brewing adheres to the notion that we take our first sip with our eyes. The food menu is small, but food trucks offer heftier fare. Stylistically, the beer is all over the map, from German lagers to Scottish ales to decidedly American IPAs, and no particular specialties other than their Kumquat IPA. When the weather is nice and the roll-up door is open, it's one of the nicest places to drink beer in Eastern Washington. **1025 S. Perry St., #2, Spokane | perrystreetbrewing.com**

OREGON

Long a hotbed for craft beer, Oregon today is packed with groundbreaking breweries and is producing some of the most inspired beers in the country. The state's devotion to artisanal processes, its support of small creative industries, and its proximity to ingredients such as hops, barley, and fruit make it a perfect storm of craft-beer ingenuity.

BEST SPOTS FOR OLD SCHOOL BEER STYLES

Heater Allen's lager fixation makes it perfect for those looking for tight, crisp, and flavorful renditions of traditional German beer styles. And Hair of the Dog Brewing Company was brewing Belgian- and German-style beers with their open direct-fire mash tun long before it was "cool."

BEST SPOTS FOR NEW SCHOOL BEER STYLES

De Garde Brewing's dedication to spontaneous fermentation is both old school and fresh in execution and focus, while Great Notion's approach to culinary-inspired kettle sours and hazy IPAs dripping with new school hops fruitiness is definitely worth a visit.

BEST SPOTS TO ENJOY A MEAL WITH YOUR BEER

Deschutes Brewpub's fare is just as great as their beers, while Block 15 Brewing's restaurant serves up delicious gastropub dishes.

MOST STYLISH TAPROOMS AND BARS

Buoy Beer Co.'s see-through floor lets you watch the walruses hanging out below the pier while you wait for a table in the bustling brewpub, and Logsdon Farmhouse Ales' location on a beautiful farm with a stunning view of Mount Hood is hard to beat.

MOST AWARD-WINNING BREWERIES

Pelican Pub & Brewery's 39 GABF and 19 World Beer Cup medals are a testament to the quality of their beer, while Rogue's 29 GABF and 11 WBC medals reflect the unyielding field-to-glass focus of brewmaster John Maier.

BEST UNIQUE BEER EXPERIENCE

Blairally Vintage Arcade has one of Eugene's best tap lists and a cool collection of vintage pinball machines, while Sassy's in Portland is both one-of-a-kind and definitely NSFW. For a more grounded experience, visit Rogue Farms and see where the beer is grown.

PORTLAND

It's no surprise that Portland, a city of now 53 registered breweries, attracts some thirsty travelers. With beer tourism at a peak, Portland is getting the spotlight not only for its classic brewpubs that got the microbrew ball rolling in the 1980s, but also for its growing number of smaller niche breweries that focus on specific styles of beer and brewing methods.

CRYSTAL BALLROOM: Brothers Mike and Brian McMenamin opened their first Oregon pub in 1974 and have since opened more than 50 restaurants and brewpubs in historic buildings throughout the Northwest. Among their Portland venues are the Crystal Ballroom concert hall in downtown Portland. **1332 W Burnside St., Portland | mcmenamins.com/ Crystal Ballroom**

BAGDAD THEATER AND PUB/BACKSTAGE BAR: Another venue by the McMenmins is their Portland pub, the Bagdad Theater and Pub with the attached Backstage Bar on Hawthorne Street. The theater shows first-run movies and serves pizza, popcorn, and candy, in addition to the beers on tap. The Backstage Bar is where you can sip on a beer while playing pool, shuffleboard, and pinball, listen to live music, and relax. Pets are allowed at the sidewalk seating area, too! **3702 SE Hawthorne Blvd., Portland | Theater: mcmenamins.com/219-bagdad-theater-pub-home; Bar: mcmenamins.com/603-back-stage-bar-home**

KENNEDY SCHOOL: A renovated elementary school in northeast Portland that's a lot like a craft-beer maze, the Kennedy School features different bars, a restaurant, and a brewery throughout the school halls and classrooms. The Kennedy School is also a hotel with 57 rooms, some of which still have the original chalkboards intact. Check out the stunning outdoor soaking pool. **5736 NE 33rd Ave., Portland | mcmenamins. com/KennedySchool**

BREAKSIDE BREWERY: Winning a GABF gold medal in the IPA category is hard—as a category, it routinely packs the most entries of any category in the competition. So when Breakside won not only gold for their IPA but also a bronze for their Wanderlust IPA (in the strong pale ale category) in 2014, it put the beer world on notice. But these accolades weren't new—they had won numerous medals in styles ranging from sour to stout to traditional German and traditional English. Today, a visit to either Breakside location (the brewpub or the Milwaukie production brewery and tasting room) offers about two dozen of their own beers on tap, and it's hard to go wrong with any beer in any style. We can vouch for everything from their Pilsner to Safeword triple IPA, and their Salted Caramel Stout is a sessionable favorite. **Brewpub: 820 NE Dekum St., Portland / Brewery: 5821 SE International Wy., Milwaukie | breakside.com**

BRIDGEPORT BREWING: Originally called Columbia River Brewery and renamed after one of Portland's first microbrews, Bridgeport Ale, Bridgeport Brewing is one of, if not the, iconic Portland brewpub. Guests can now enjoy the company's big hops-forward flagships such as the classic IPA and the Hop Czar imperial IPA or the double fresh-hopped Pilsner High Hop at the brewery and ale house in the Pearl District. **1313**

NW Marshall St., Portland | bridgeportbrew.com

CASCADE BREWING BARREL HOUSE: Cascade is the leader of Portland's sour beer movement with barrel-aged, fruit-infused beers. Cascade has a tap system that draws beer directly from the barrel into guests' glasses. Expect funky beers such as Sang Noir, a red ale-double red ale blend aged in bourbon and pinot noir barrels for 12 to 24 months and then blended again with barrel-aged Bing and sour pie cherries. The brewery also makes seasonal blueberry, strawberry, and apricot sours. **939**

SE Belmont St., Portland | cascadebrewingbarrelhouse.com

WIDMER BROS. BREWING: Another duo of brothers known as godfathers of Portland's brewpub scene are Kurt and Rob Widmer, who opened in 1984. They opened with traditional German-style beers, a weizenbier and an altbier, and would go on to create some of Portland's first seasonal beers. Widmer also helped found the Oregon Brewer's Festival, now the largest outdoor craft-beer festival in the country. The Widmer brewery still produces its classic beers, seasonals, experimental batches, and a line of gluten-free beer called Omission at its location on North Russell Street. **929**

N. Russell St., Portland | widmerbrothers.com

COMMONS BREWERY: (Below) Originally opened as Beetje Brewery in owner Mike Wright's garage, Commons began one barrel at a time. Wright was a passionate homebrewer who wanted to make easy-drinking French and Belgian-inspired beers. Beetje is Dutch for "a little bit," but they were growing, and it wasn't a little bit so they moved into a commercial space

and launched Commons Brewery. Portlanders and visitors have been gathering around the 8 rotating taps at Commons, where they can enjoy the beers just steps away from where they are brewed under the watchful eye of head brewer Sean Burke. The Belgian, French, and now German theme still unites the lineup, to which they have been adding some inventive ingredients. For example, the Flemish Kiss Belgian pale ale uses Alt yeast in primary fermentation, and the sour Beer Royale's yeast comes from the live *Lactobacillus* that Burke cultivated from Nancy's yogurt (a local Portland company). **630 SE Belmont St., Portland | commonsbrewery.com**

APEX: A BEER BAR: If you love beer, you should visit Apex, no questions asked. It's cozy indoors, but when the weather allows, the patio more than doubles capacity, which is necessary to accommodate the throngs of serious and regular beer fans that flock to their 50 taps of awesomeness. When they're busy, it's not the kind of place where you'll have an in-depth discussion with the bartender—know what you want, order quickly, and make space for the next person at the bar—but what the bar lacks in hand-holding, it more than makes up for in awesome beer served quickly and efficiently in a vibrant and energetic space. **1216 SE Division St., Portland | apexbar.com**

HAIR OF THE DOG BREWING COMPANY: Owner and Brewer Alan Sprints has been brewing interesting, mainly Belgian- and German-inspired beers, since 1993—long before it was "cool." Big beers such as Adam, Fred, and Matt are built to be savored, and the many variations on these (including barrel-aged editions) served in the tap room are ideal for sharing with friends. The limited food menu is really, really good, and the high-ceilinged industrial space is comfortable with a large wraparound bar. Don't pass up the opportunity to take a tour with Sprints—from his open mash tun to concrete fermentor, he's both committed to tradition and pushing the envelope, all at the same time. **61 SE Yamhill St., Portland | hairofthedog.com**

OCCIDENTAL BREWING: This Portland brewery specializes in German-style lagers and puts on an annual German food and beer festival, the Humbug Lager Fest. Find the full lineup of beers in the tap room, take a tour of the brewery, and have your growler or corny keg filled. **6635 N. Baltimore Ave., Portland | occidentalbrewing.com**

GROUNDBREAKER BREWING & GASTROPUB: This southeast Portland brewery focuses exclusively on gluten-free beers that they brew with powdered chestnuts and oats. Their gastropub's food fare is also gluten-free. They source the ingredients for their beers and their food as locally as possible. **2030 SE 7th Ave., Portland | groundbreakerbrewing.com**

UPRIGHT BREWING: Another niche brewery in Portland, in the basement of the Left Bank building on North Broadway. The small brewery's taps sit on the wall next to a record player, and visitors post up among brewing equipment and barrels to try their farmhouse-style ales, notably the core saisons—the Four, Five, Six, and Seven. **240 N. Broadway, #2, Portland | uprightbrewing.com**

THE BEERMONGERS: This is a small bottle shop that has a carefully curated selection of more than 600 bottles from across the globe and eight rotating taps. They offer regular tasting events and can fill growlers and order kegs. **1125 SE Division St., Portland | thebeermongers.com**

BELMONT STATION: Belmont is an infamous bottle shop and tavern that has more than 1,200 bottles, an adjacent bar called Biercafé with 20 taps, and a beer engine. Kegs are available to go, and their kitchen offers sandwiches, salads, and snacks. Frequent tasting events and meet-the-brewer events are posted on the website. **4500 SE Stark St., Portland | belmont-station.com**

HOP & VINE: Brunch at a bottle shop? Say no more. This north Portland hub has a full bar, an impressive bottle selection, and the best bottle-shop food in town. Their food menu offers apps, salads, soups, brunch, and desserts, and if you want something besides beer you can order from their wine and signature cocktails menu. **1914 N. Killingsworth St., Portland |**
thehopandvine.com

SARAVEZA BOTTLE SHOP & PASTRY TAVERN: With more than 250 bottles and 10 taps to choose from, as well as Midwest-style pastries, Saraveza has all its bases covered. Select from easy-drinking beer to rare beer to experimental beer—there's something for everyone here. Check out their website for their busy schedule of events. **1004 N. Killingsworth St.,**
Portland | saraveza.com

HORSE BRASS PUB: Authenticity is the name of the game at Horse Brass, and publican Don Younger is a favorite of brewers for his attention to detail. The beer selection is impeccable, the service is top notch, and the atmosphere alone would be a reason to visit. The tap list will satisfy tastes from English-style cask ale to the dankest of IPAs. **4534 SE Belmont St.,**
Portland | horsebrass.com

HOPWORKS URBAN BREWERY (HUB): Don't let the name fool you— while HUB loves their hoppy beers, they're just as adept at maltier styles, too. With two locations (Powell and Bikebar) and a third coming just across the river in Vancouver, Washington, it's what you'd expect when you think of beer in Portland—quirky, fun, thoughtful, values-driven, and an overall rewarding experience. **2944 SE Powell Blvd., Portland / 3947 N, Williams Ave., Portland / 17707 SE Mill Plain Blvd., Vancouver, WA | hopworksbeer.com**

BAILEY'S TAPROOM AND THE UPPER LIP: With 25 rotating taps of craft ales, lagers, and ciders, Bailey's comfortable tap room is perfect for downtown pub crawlers as well as the after-work crowd. Or you can visit Bailey's second-floor "secret" bar, The Upper Lip. If you walk around the corner from Bailey's to a door marked with a bottle and up a flight of stairs, you'll find a room just as large as the first floor, 6 taps, and a huge case of bottles. **213 SW Broadway, Portland / 720 SW Ankeny St., Portland | baileystaproom.com / baileystaproom.com/the-upper-lip**

GREAT NOTION BREWING: A newcomer on the scene, Great Notion started with gusto in early 2016 and has taken the Portland beer world by storm with their creative sour beers and progressively hopped New England-style IPAs. If you want a beer that tastes like pancakes, try the Double Stack imperial stout (with maple syrup). If you want a sour beer that tastes like dessert, try the Key Lime Pie Berliner Weisse. And if you want the IPA that Portlanders in 2016 voted the best of the city, try their Juicebox IPA. And don't miss the food—it holds its own amid the massively flavorful beer. **2204 NE Alberta St., #101, Portland | greatnotionpdx.com**

FAT HEAD'S BREWERY: This PNW outpost of the Cleveland, Ohio-based brewery offers local hopheads yet another killer option. Their Hop Juju Imperial IPA is something else, and with two Great American Beer Festival golds plus a World Beer Cup gold, it dominates one of the toughest categories around. But you don't have to be a hophead to enjoy a great beer at Fat Head's—everything from their accessible Blueberry Wheat to their German-style beers is expertly crafted, and the restaurant pub fare is above average. **131 NW 13th Ave., Portland | fatheadsportland.com**

ECLIPTIC BREWING: Founder and Brewer John Harris made his mark on Oregon beer at a number of other breweries—McMenamins, Deschutes, Full Sail—but Ecliptic is his chance to call his own shots and make the beers he wants to make. The warehouse brewery is simple, the food is solid, and the beers (pardon the astronomy pun) are out of this world. **825 N. Cook St., Portland | eclipticbrewing.com**

EX NOVO BREWING CO.: Do-gooders doing good, one beer at a time. Ex Novo is a nonprofit and donates 100 percent of net profits to charitable causes at home and around the world, meaning every pint you buy not only makes you happy, but makes the world a better place. **2326 N. Flint Ave., Portland | exnovobrew.com**

BURNSIDE BREWING COMPANY: We made a visit to Burnside during the Craft Brewers Conference in 2015, when the beer-writers guild gathered there for their bi-annual meeting. The beers were simple yet tasty, the food was solid, and it's a great place to drink if you're looking for dinner and not just a couple pints. **701 E. Burnside St., Portland | burnsidebrewco.com**

SASSY'S: We're not exactly sure why Portland is so associated with "gentlemen's clubs," but Sassy's is an institution, and the beer selection is excellent (almost 30 beers on tap and more in bottles). During happy hour, all beers are $2.50. Order a Boneyard RPM on tap, grab a seat near the stage, and enjoy the scene. **927 SE Morrison St., Portland | www.sassysbar.com**

LOYAL LEGION PUB: With 99 taps, most serving Oregon craft beers on the weekends, sausages house-made or sourced from Portland's

Olympia Provisions, pretzels from ChefStable's house bakery, Philippe's Bread, what more can you ask of a beer hall? At the Loyal Legion, they are definitely out to celebrate the Oregon craft-beer tradition. Order an award-winning hoppy creation from Barley Brown's, pFreim, Breakside, or Block 15. Or taste Ninkasi's Bourbon Barrel-Aged Ground Control brewed with Oregon hazelnuts, star anise, and cocoa nibs, and fermented with Ninkasi's "space yeast." Take home a growler of Boneyard Diablo Rojo.

710 SE 6th Ave., Portland | loyallegionpdx.com

HONORABLE MENTION: The four Lucky Labrador Brewing Company locations (luckylab.com) are almost institutions in Portland—favorite spots to take out-of-town guests. The beer itself isn't something you'll write home about, but there's just something about Lucky Lab that feels so Portland, we couldn't not include them.

HOOD RIVER

Located in the heart of the Columbia River Gorge, with Mt. Hood looming over, Hood River is among the most scenic destinations for a pint in the state.

FULL SAIL BREWING CO.: As the 27-year-old veteran of the bunch, Full Sail should be the starting point for a Hood River journey. The downtown pub is bustling at noon on a Friday, both inside the cozy bar and on the outdoor deck overlooking the Gorge, and they're pouring a selection of Full Sail favorites, such as their Session Lagers, and pub exclusives, such as the Passport Lager, a Dortmunder Export style. Take a tour, then try one of their many beers on tap, order a bite to eat, or take a keg or growler to go!

506 Columbia St., Hood River | fullsailbrewing.com

PFRIEM FAMILY BREWERS: Located in a commercial space along the waterfront, the brewery has made a name for itself in Hood River and beyond with their Belgian-inspired, Northwest hops-infused ales. The juicy 7.2 percent IPA seems to be the favorite, but they execute a range of styles, from the Schwarzbier to a Wit. Take one of their Belgian-inspired dishes and a pint to the outdoor area, which features a fire pit for lounging and a view of the Gorge, then take a growler to go. **707 Portway Ave., #101, Hood River | pfriembeer.com**

DOUBLE MOUNTAIN BREWERY: A fresh-hops heaven during the harvest season, between returning favorites Killer Green, brewed with Brewer's Gold hops variety from Sodbuster Farms, and Killer Red, featuring Perle and Sterling hops also from Sodbuster, and fresh hops one-offs such as Mörder Weizen, brewed with wheat and fresh Magnum hops and fermented with a Kölsch yeast. Their 16-inch New Haven–style pizza pies pair perfectly with a fresh-hops ale, and you can get bottles and growlers to go. **8 Fourth St., Hood River | doublemountainbrewery.com**

LOGSDON FARMHOUSE ALES: After a meandering journey along vine-yard- and orchard-lined roads outside Hood River, you arrive at the bucolic bliss of Logsdon Farmhouse Ales, where you can enjoy earthy, rustic ales, such as their Seizoen and Seizoen Brett, in a true farmhouse setting. Funky and sour offerings, such as the Far West Vlaming, a Flanders red–style ale, and Half Naked Spring Break, a collaboration with nearby Solera Brewery, are also a treat. Sip samples in the rustic tasting room while overlooking the horses drinking from a pond and a stellar view of Mount Hood. They have a tasting room at Logsdon Barrel House & Taproom, too, featuring beers on tap and traditional Belgian fare. **Farm: 4785 Booth Hill Rd., Hood River | farmhousebeer.com / Taproom: 101 4th St., Hood River | logsdonbarrelhouse.com**

MT. HOOD

MT. HOOD BREWING CO: Don't miss the powder on Mt. Hood or one of their 8 fresh craft beer-offerings on tap. The casual, family-friendly venue offers a full menu of pizzas, sandwiches, and more. **87304 Government Camp Loop, Government Camp | mthoodbrewing.com**

WILLAMETTE VALLEY

WOLVES & PEOPLE FARMHOUSE BREWERY: (Below) Forty-five minutes outside of Portland in wine country, this little farmhouse brewery is located on Founder Christian DeBenedetti's family farm. The beers are primarily funky takes on the farmhouse genre—farmhouse pales and saisons—and wild ales made with their own house yeast they call Sebastian that was isolated on a fruit tree in their orchard. Try the Instinctive Travels dry-hopped farmhouse ale (it's to farmhouse ales what New England-style IPA is to IPA) or the light and crisp Landbouw grisette. **30203 NE Benjamin Rd., Newberg | wolvesandpeople.com**

HEATER ALLEN BREWING: These lager fanatics brew some of the best in Oregon (roughly a dozen different varieties throughout the year). As a brewer, you have to love what you do to brew lagers on this scale, as the time and tank space they require is hard to justify in monetary terms. But the result is beer styles that few other brewers produce, executed beautifully. While the taproom is only open on Fridays and Saturdays, their beer is easy to find at better beer bars in Portland. **907 NE 10th Ave., McMinnville | heaterallen.com**

BLOCK 15 BREWING COMPANY: Their mini-empire in Corvallis consists of two locations—the original downtown brewpub with a 7-barrel brewhouse and the production brewery with a 20-barrel brewhouse and packaging lines. Beer-wise, their Sticky Hands DIPA packs a ton of dank lupulin punch, and their expanding sour-beer program is paying dividends. The lengthy gastropub menu at the restaurant and brewery is great if you're hungry, while the smaller sandwich-centric menu at the production brewery taproom hits the spot when your focus is primarily on the beer. **300 SW Jefferson Ave., Corvallis / 3415 SW Deschutes St., Corvallis | block15.com**

ROGUE FARMS: Rogue is everywhere in Oregon, but Rogue Farms in Independence gets to the very soul of the brewery—this is where the hops in their beer are grown, the barley in their beer is harvested, the honeybees that make their honey colonized. Plenty of breweries use the term "farm-to-glass" but Rogue is the only brewery in the United States to take it this far and raises their own ingredients in genuinely sustainable ways on this kind of scale. It's a beautiful sight to behold, and speaks to how they are just as focused on values as they are on beer quality and community. **3590 Wigrich Rd., Independence | roguefarms.com**

WESTERN OREGON

TERMINAL GRAVITY BREWING CO.: If exploring the mountains is your thing, head east and stop by Terminal Gravity while you're there. They've been brewing since 1997, but they're not afraid to take the leap into new beers when the market asks for them. Case in point, their new Citra-driven Eagle Cap IPA flagship. When you're ready for some adventure, the brewpub is open 7 days a week. **803 E. 4th St., Enterprise | terminalgravitybrewing.com**

EUGENE

NINKASI BREWING COMPANY: Located in Eugene's funky Whiteaker neighborhood, the brewery has built its reputation with hops, presenting the market with a robust lineup of ales. Although the Ninkasi beer lineup is characteristically bold and hoppy, the brewery has demonstrated its versatility with beers such as Spring Reign, an English-style session beer, and the Pravda Bohemian Pils, a spicy, medium-bodied Pilsner. Take one of their daily tours, then head to the tasting room—outside food is allowed, so bring your own, order in, or catch one of their daily food carts. Kids are allowed until 8 p.m. with an adult. Kegs and corny fills are available. **272 Van Buren St., Eugene | ninkasibrewing.com**

BLAIRALLY VINTAGE ARCADE: Come for the vintage arcade, but stay for the craft-beer offerings. The barcade has a sweet devotion to pre-serving, refurbishing, and sharing vintage gaming within its community, all while boasting one of the town's best tap lists. Their Facebook page has a lineup of nightly events, including games, music, dancing, and DJs. **245 Blair Blvd., Eugene | facebook.com/blairallyarcade**

AGRARIAN ALES: Agrarian is producing ales from hops and herbs grown on-site at Crossroads Farm and soon will grow its own grains to claim estate-brewery status. This family-friendly venue offers a rotating lineup of beers, farm-fresh food, games, live music, and a beer garden. You can bring your dog, too! Nestled on 4 acres in the heart of the green Willamette Valley, this is one destination you don't want to miss. **31115 Crossroads Ln. W., Eugene | agales.com**

OAKSHIRE BREWING: Well-brewed, authentic, artisanal beer in a comfortable tap room fed by rotating food trucks. Oakshire's higher profile releases, such as the barrel-aged Hellshire beers, are great, but don't miss out on their deliciously sessionable core beers such as the 5.8 percent ABV Overcast Espresso Stout. **1055 Madera St., Eugene | oakbrew.com**

FALLING SKY BREWING HOUSE & GASTROPUB: Brewery, deli, pizzeria, homebrew shop. The brewing entrepreneurs behind Falling Sky are ambitious, if nothing else. The food is as good as the beers, with house-cured meats and a taste of East Coast love in this Eugene favorite. **1334 Oak Alley, Eugene | fallingskybrewing.com**

THE BIER STEIN BOTTLE SHOP & PUB: Dine and drink in, or grab bottles to go from the massive selection of great beer at the Bier Stein. The selection is enormous—the best around. **1591 Willamette St., Eugene | thebierstein.com**

OAKRIDGE

BREWERS UNION LOCAL 180: Located in Oakridge, a tiny moun-tain-biking town surrounded by the Cascade Range, this public house is as authentic as you can find in the United States. Its beers are designed to be served on cask (they're brewed with English Maris Otter malt and low hops). And its cozy location in the mountains makes you feel as if you're sitting amid the hills in England (albeit with a few more trees). The family friendly establishment serves up beers, food, and live music. **48329 E. 1st St., Oakridge | brewersunion.com**

OREGON COAST

FORT GEORGE BREWERY & PUBLIC HOUSE: Brewmaster Jack Harris brewed all over before settling in Astoria to open Fort George Brewery, and the beers he brews today feel just as accomplished and well-traveled. While his crew is adept at brewing stouts (Cavatica), Scot-tish ales (Plaid), and other malty styles, the real stars of the show are the hoppy beers—Vortex IPA, 3-Way IPA, Optimist IPA, Magnanimous IPA, and more. The downstairs pub offers burgers, the upstairs restaurant offers really great pizza, but no matter where you end up, the beer is delicious. **1483 Duane St., Astoria | fortgeorgebrewery.com**

BUOY BEER CO.: Right on the water in a former fish processing facility, Buoy Beer's brewing program is driven by the accomplished Kevin Shaw, an alum of Bert Grant's and Bridgeport. The beer is dialed-in, with tight renditions of popular styles and a few mean lagers that really showcase their precision. The brewpub food is equally fantastic, and you'll love the see-through floor that showcases the walruses perched on the pilings below the pier. **1 8th St., Astoria | buoybeer.com**

DE GARDE BREWING: (Following page) Trevor Rogers and wife Linsey Hamacher make a lineup of beers inspired by German and Belgian farmhouse traditions. Spontaneous fermentation (fermenting beer only with airborne wild yeast and bacteria) gives their beer a unique terroir and sense of place, and extended fermentation and aging in foeders and barrels adds even more depth of funk and flavor. Today, they're able to draw on older barrels (some 3–4 years old) in their blends, much like the Belgian masters they've modeled the brewery after. Big release weekends draw huge crowds, so if you're searching for a quieter experience, you might want to check and make sure nothing big is planned. Also, their license does not allow underage patrons on site, so you'll need to leave the little ones with a babysitter. But if you do make the trip, you're in for a treat—when discussion of the best sour beer producers in America comes up, they're always in the conversation. Embrace the slow life and surprising flavors of de Garde's native beers. **6000 Blimp Blvd., Tillamook | degardebrewing.com**

PELICAN PUB & BREWERY: This brewpub in Pacific City is one of the winningest breweries in Oregon, with 39 Great American Beer Festival medals and 19 World Beer Cup medals to their name. Even more impressive is their repeat wins for the same beers—their Tsunami Foreign Export Stout, for example, has won medals in three different decades, starting in the late 1990s and most recently in 2013. Maintaining that legacy of consistently great beer for 18+ years is no small feat. More recently, the blind panel of judges for *Craft Beer & Brewing Magazine*® rated their Mother of All Storms barrel-aged barleywine a perfect 100. If you're making the visit, sit outside if you can—the view is incredible and worth spending a few extra bucks on a burger than you normally would. If you visit during the height of the summer tourist season, be prepared to wait—grab a beer or three from the bar, and the time will pass before you know it. **33180 Cape Kiwanda Dr., Pacific City | yourlittlebeachtown.com/eat-drink/pelican-pub-brewery**

ROGUE BREWERS ON THE BAY: If Rogue Farms is the soul of Rogue Nation, Brewers On The Bay in Newport is the both the heart and the brain. This is where the rubber meets the road—where brewing maestro John Maier and his team of brewers take those ingredients and turn them into liquid gold. It's also the place to soak up Rogue history while touring the storied production brewery, via their cheekily-named "Roguesonian" museum and beerquarium. **2320 OSU Dr., Newport | rogue.com**

BEND

BONEYARD BEER: Ski beautiful Mt. Bachelor by day and visit Boneyard, Bend, Oregon's "boneyard of brewing equipment" in an old auto shop tucked away in the back streets of the downtown historical district. Don't miss the RPM IPA and the Bone-A-Fide West Coast-style Pale Ale. Spend some time in the tasting room and try one of their offerings on tap, buy some sweet swag, fill your growler, and even go home with a keg. **37 NW Lake Pl., Ste. B, Bend | boneyardbeer.com**

DESCHUTES BREWERY: When in Bend, the only question you have to ask is whether you're going to the Deschutes brewpub or the tasting room at the production brewery. Deschutes is Bend, Bend is Deschutes, and no beer-centric vacation would be complete without a visit. The pub tends to have more specialty and one-offs on tap, so if you're really wanting to geek out, that's your spot. But the free tour with free beer samples at the production brewery is hard to beat, too. Might as well do both. **Brewpub: 1044 NW Bond St., Bend / 901 SW Simpson Ave., Bend | deschutesbrewery.com**

CRUX FERMENTATION PROJECT: Former Deschutes Brewmaster Larry Sidor realized his dream to open his own brewery, and the beers are everything you'd expect—intensely creative, vividly flavorful, wildly diverse. No style is off limits, from Pilsner to oud bruin, and the comfortable and modern taproom exudes a rooted but contemporary style. You can't go wrong ordering here—grab a Half Hitch DIPA if hops are your game, a Freakcake wild ale if you're in the mood for some pucker, or a Pilz if you want something light and sessionable.
50 SW Division St., Bend | cruxfermentation.com

10 BARREL BREWING: We try to avoid the politics of craft beer—10 Barrel's sale to AB-Inbev a couple years ago was polarizing, to say the least—but one thing we can say is that they're still putting out beer at the same (or better) quality than before the acquisition (no matter how much critics on the Internet might think they can taste some mythical difference). We're big fans of Joe IPA, and the Cucumber Crush sour is really something else. **Brewery: 62970 NE 18th St., Bend / Pub: 135 NW Galveston, Bend | 10barrel.com**

THE ALE APOTHECARY: Creative, mixed-fermentation wild beers are the name of the game at Ale Apothecary. But don't try to visit—their very small-scale operation is as artisanal as artisanal gets, and they'd rather spend their limited time making beer rather than staffing a taproom. However, when you're out and about at local Bend bottle shops such as Broken Top Bottle Shop (btbsbend.com) or The Brew Shop (thebrewshopbend .com), do yourself a favor and grab a bottle to take home and share with friends. **61517 River Rd., Bend | thealeapothecary.com**

THE BREW SHOP: Homebrew shop, 500+ beer retail selection, and craft-beer pub—what's not to like? The love of craft beer is evident at The Brew Shop, so stop in and grab some hard-to-find to-go bottles, and grab a pint at the bar while you're there. **1203 NE Third St., Bend | thebrewshopbend.com**

BAKER CITY

BARLEY BROWN'S PUB & BREWERY: Looking at Barley Brown's restaurant from the outside, you might not expect much, but one taste of the beer will change your mind. Hops are at the top of the menu—Pallet Jack IPA, Hand Truck Pale Ale, Forklift DIPA, Headshake DIPA, and the rest are all amazing expression of lupulin artistry. The pub grub is solid and the non-hoppy beers should not be overlooked. If you're looking for a more beer-centric experience without the food angle, check out the brewery taphouse, one block away. **Restaurant: 2190 Main St., Baker City | Taphouse: 2200 Main St., Baker City | barleybrownsbeer.com**

CALIFORNIA

The largest state in the nation (based on population) is also host to the largest number of craft brewers, with more than 600 operational breweries at last count. From wild ales brewed in Wine Country up north to wood-fermented English-style pub ales on the Central Coast and San Diego County's hop-centricity, there's plenty of ground to explore for intrepid craft-beer adventurers.

BEST SPOTS FOR OLD SCHOOL BEER STYLES

Firestone Walker's Burton Union-style fermentation for DBA (below right) is as classic as it gets (despite their very new-school approach to other beers), while MacLeod's Ale House's focus on traditional English-style cask ales served on hand-pulled beer engines is historic and refreshing.

BEST SPOTS FOR NEW SCHOOL BEER STYLES

The Bruery in Orange County has scaled their program of spirits barrel–aged beers to impressive heights, and their Black Tuesday, Chocolate Rain, and Grey Monday stouts are legendary. In the Bay Area, Cellarmaker, The Rare Barrel, and Sante Adairius are all must-visits.

BEST SPOTS TO ENJOY A MEAL WITH YOUR BEER

The Russian River brewpub is an absolute must for a meal and beer—they're as fanatical about service and hospitality as they are about their beer (and who can pass up a great pub meal with a glass of ultra-fresh Pliny?); Waypoint Public (above right) pairs amazing food with great beer.

MOST STYLISH TAPROOMS AND BARS

Both Modern Times locations have the artsy hipster angle on lock—they're cool without being intimidating. Every Firestone Walker tap room and restaurant is an expression of the intense care and attention to detail you'd expect from such an award-winning brewery.

MOST AWARD-WINNING BREWERIES

Firestone Walker's 47 GABF medals and 25 WBC medals put them in the upper stratosphere of winningest breweries, while Pizza Port Carlsbad, Russian River Brewing, Figueroa Mountain, Beachwood Brewing, Marin Brewing, and Alesmith have also made strong showings.

BEST UNIQUE BEER EXPERIENCE

We've never seen anything like the multiple in-depth tour options at Sierra Nevada Brewing, where participants can not only celebrate the history of this groundbreaking brewery but also get an incredibly in-depth look at how they make beer, from expertly trained tour guides.

SAN DIEGO

Odds are that you've enjoyed a beer brewed in San Diego, even if you weren't aware of it. Since the 1990s, this Southern California brewing stronghold has built a worldwide reputation for great beer, anchored by now-classic craft brewers such as Stone, Lost Abbey/Port Brewing, Green Flash, Ballast Point, AleSmith, Karl Strauss, and others. But in addition to these widely distributed powerhouses, San Diego County has also cultivated one of the strongest local beer scenes around, with eighty-seven licensed breweries and brewpubs, plus another thirty-three in planning.

To the uninitiated, this sounds like an enormous, and unsustainable, number. But one visit to San Diego and it all makes sense—the city loves craft beer; the breweries reach different customers in a variety of areas with individual specialties; and self-respecting beer tourists could entertain themselves for days without drinking the same beer (or brewery, for that matter) twice.

NORTH PARK/NORMAL HEIGHTS

San Diego's breweries are best enjoyed neighborhood by neighborhood, and North Park is a great place to start for a number of great beer options within walking distance of each other.

MIKE HESS BREWING: At Mike Hess Brewing's North Park location, the gleaming brewhouse and fermentors are on display below as you enter the tasting room through a catwalk. Try their World Beer Cup gold-winning Habitus Rye IPA and grab a spot at one of the communal tables. **3812 Grim Ave., San Diego | mikehessbrewing.com**

WAYPOINT PUBLIC: The quality of the food from Executive Chef Amanda Baumgarten (a former Top Chef contestant) at Waypoint Public is matched only by the depth of their beer list, curated by Bottlecraft Owner Brian Jensen. **3794 30th St., San Diego | waypointpublic.com**

BOTTLECRAFT NORTH PARK: This retail location is a perfect after-dinner stop. Their cold cases are atypically arranged by beer style and offer a tempting selection of some of the best beers available in California. **3007 University Ave., San Diego | store.bottlecraftbeer.com**

RIP CURRENT BREWING NORTH PARK TASTING ROOM: This brewery was named Very Small Brewing Company and Brewer of the Year at the 2015 Great American Beer Festival. At their new tasting room in North Park, you can enjoy one of their highly rated IPAs (such as the Lupulin Lust) or go for something darker, such as their Vanilla Storm imperial porter. **1325 Grand Ave., #100, San Marcos / 4101 30th St. (Intersection with Polk Ave.), San Diego | ripcurrentbrewing.com**

THE HOMEBREWER: A well-designed supply and resource shop with helpful staff focused on great customer service. They have built out a test brewery in the space next to the shop where they can work with split batches for experiments with brewing techniques and ingredients. **2911 El Cajon Blvd., #2, San Diego | thehomebrewersd.com**

TIGER! TIGER!: Has a tap list and menu that have rightfully earned it spots on others' top beer bars lists (no surprise, as it's co-owned by a former brewer for Stone Brewing Co.). If you're limited for time, it's a great

place to sample everything from Societe's The Harlot to Alpine's Pure Hoppiness. **3025 El Cajon Blvd., San Diego | tigertigertavern.blogspot.com**

BLIND LADY ALE HOUSE: (above) Tiger! Tiger!'s sister bar is an iconic drinking destination offering Neapolitan-style pizza, 26 beers on tap, and an impressive selection of bottles and cans. It is also home to Automatic Brewing Co., a 10-barrel brewery operated by Blind Lady's owner, who formerly worked at Stone Brewing Co. **3416 Adams Ave., San Diego | blindlady.blogspot.com**

MODERN TIMES BREWING NORTH PARK FLAVORDOME: On the south end of North Park, this establishment offers a walkable remote tap room for their Point Loma brewery. Fortunate Islands hoppy wheat beer makes for a perfectly sessionable and flavorful afternoon beer. **3000 Upas St. (corner of 30th & Upas), San Diego | moderntimesbeer.com/tasting-room/north-park**

FALL BREWING: An alum of St. Archer and Mission, Cofounder and Brewer Ramon Astamendi can finally call his own shots at Fall. The result is punchy small beers—most under 6 percent ABV—that pack in a lot of flavor while remaining imminently drinkable. Says a lot that their flagship, if you can call it that, is a Pilsner. Killer open warehouse vibe, excellent soundtrack, and fantastic beers—what more could you ask for?

4542 30th St., San Diego | fallbrewing.com

PANAMA 66: Opened by the people behind esteemed beer bars Tiger! Tiger! and Blind Lady Ale House, Panama 66 is among the most scenic spots to grab a beer. Located in Balboa Park at the San Diego Museum of Art, Panama 66 lets visitors enjoy a pint from some of San Diego's best, such as Alpine, Societe, and Lost Abbey, and a sandwich or a salad in the laid-back courtyard bar adjacent to the museum. The menu includes beer and cocktails paired with, or inspired by, pieces of art, and you can finish the meal with a walk around one of Balboa Park's many beautiful gardens.

1450 El Prado, San Diego | panama66.blogspot.com

GASLAMP QUARTER AND LITTLE ITALY

CORONADO BREWING: From Stingray IPA to Barrel-aged Stupid Stout, we've been mighty impressed with the beers coming out of Coronado Brewing. Visit the brewpub out on Coronado Island and take the ferry from the convention center or Broadway pier for a bit of extra local flavor. **170 Orange Ave., Coronado | coronadobrewing.com**

MONKEY PAW BREWING: With a nice mix of their own brews and an impressive lineup of guest beers, Monkey Paw will please everyone in your party. Fun collabs with star California brewers mean there's always something new and exciting on the menu. **805 16th St., San Diego | monkeypawbrewing.com**

HALF DOOR BREWING CO.: Historical downtown building reinvented as a brewery and pub. Full menu, classic aesthetic, solid beers across standard styles, and right next to Petco Park—a fun stop if you're in the area. **903 Island Ave., San Diego | halfdoorbrewing.com**

MISSION BREWERY: Mission Brewery is located in what was once a Wonder Bread factory. Built in 1894, the building still has several of the same architectural features, such as bow trusses, that came with the original building. The brewery features a 2,500-square-foot tasting room, food trucks that visit almost every day, and beers that have won numerous national and international awards. And if you decide to take a tour, kids and dogs are welcome. **1441 L St., San Diego | missionbrewery.com**

HONORABLE MENTION: The Little Italy location of Ballast Point (ballast point.com/locations) is home to their small-scale pilot brewery and a rather large tap room with plenty of patio space for soaking up the San Diego sun. The casual counter service kitchen is remarkably good, and the beer... well, you already know how great that is; Bottlecraft's Littly Italy location (store .bottlecraftbeer.com/pages/little-italy) is just down the block from Ballast Point and an attractive way to shop for great bottles; You'll find all of your favorites at the Stone Brewing Outpost in San Diego Airport's Terminal 2 (stonebrewing.com/visit/outposts/airport), but if Arrogant Bastard, Ruination, and Levitation aren't reasons enough to stop in, then the chimichurri steak sandwich with cilantro aioli is. You can buy bombers to take home.

MID-COUNTY

A short drive from San Diego proper puts you in what might very well be one of the greatest concentrations of breweries and beer-related businesses in the country.

ALESMITH BREWING COMPANY: The gorgeous new brewery and tap room offer a variety of experiences not possible in the old—a Tony Gwinn museum, a barrel blending bar where you can custom blend your own beers from their barrel-aged offerings, and more. The chance to try Barrel-aged Speedway Stout on tap is alone worth the visit. But, to be frank, Peter Zien and company are almost incapable of making beer that isn't delicious. We're glad that they now have a lot more space to make a lot more beer. **9990 AleSmith Ct., San Diego | alesmith.com**

BALLAST POINT BREWING COMPANY: (left) This brewery and restaurant is absolutely stunning. The ultramodern nautical theme carries throughout, and every detail was considered—they even have heaters underneath the beautiful outdoor deck to make it comfortable year round. The food is fantastic, the beer is out of this world, and the overall experience of quality is one of the best in all of craft beer. **9045 Carroll Wy., San Diego | ballastpoint.com**

SAINT ARCHER BREWING CO.: If you enjoy your beer with a hefty dose of skateboarding, surfing, or snowboarding, pop in for a taste of this rapidly growing brand. Now a part of the MillerCoors Tenth & Blake portfolio, it's not quite the antiestablishment entity portrayed in its earlier days, but the beer is still satisfying. **9550 Distribution Ave., San Diego | saintarcherbrewery.com**

WHITE LABS: Homebrewers won't want to miss the tasting room, where the in-house brewery splits batches and serves taster trays of the same recipe pitched with different yeasts. Their 32 taps of experiments with yeast and souring bacteria might keep you busy until closing time. **9495 Candida St., San Diego | whitelabs.com/tasting-room**

GREEN FLASH BREWING CO: Here, you'll find 30 taps filled with everything from its classic West Coast IPA to barrel-aged Belgian-style beers and special one-offs from its "Genius Lab." Added bonus—the chance to try all the beers from Alpine (now a part of Green Flash) without having to drive out into the mountains. **6550 Mira Mesa Blvd., San Diego | greenflashbrew.com**

BENCHMARK BREWING: (right) This is where former AleSmith Head Brewer (and QUAFF Homebrew club member) Matt Akin and his wife, Rachel, have been brewing up very tasty and sessionable brews for the past couple of years. Their Belgian-style table beer delivers on flavor at a very modest 4 percent ABV, and their oatmeal stout is rich and full-bodied while only clocking in at 4.5 percent ABV. **6190 Fairmount Ave., San Diego | benchmarkbrewing.com**

SOCIETE BREWING: (below) This brewery has carved out an enormous tap room, brewery, and barrel cellar in Kearny Mesa and is quickly building an impeccable reputation for its hoppy, Belgian-inspired, and dark beers. Their Pugilist Irish Dry Stout won silver at the 2014 World Beer Cup, and The Pupil West Coast–style IPA and The Harlot Belgian-style pale are frequent guests on the tap lists of serious beer bars around San Diego. They brew IPAs more than any other style, offering up a diverse variety of IPA styles. IPAs aside, expect to find a handful of the other available styles on tap, too. Pay a visit to their tasting room and find around 15 beers on tap—Societe believes above all, fresh is best. Food trucks are onsite most days, and each night of the week offers a themed event. Kids and pets are welcome, so long as they're supervised and leashed. **8262 Clairemont Mesa Blvd., San Diego | societebrewing.com**

COUNCIL BREWING: A 3-barrel nanobrewery that hit the ground running in 2014, and their Gavel Drop IPA quickly built a following—no small feat in a town known for its IPAs. Owners Curtis and Liz Chism have a passion for mixed-fermentation beers, and their Beatitude fruit saisons are always fun while their Les Saisons oak barrel–aged saison is simply divine. **7705 Convoy Ct., San Diego | councilbrew.com**

HONORABLE MENTIONS: Grab a pint at the San Diego location of Toronado (toronadosd.com), and you'll discover a much better behaved tap room than their raucous San Francisco location but a similarly great tap list nonetheless. Hamilton's Tavern (hamiltonstavern.com) is dark and intimate—it'll take a second for your eyes to adjust coming in from the San Diego sun—but the tap list is killer, and it's earned its classic status.

NORTH COUNTY

STONE BREWING CO.: No trip to San Diego would be complete without experiencing the Stone Brewing Co. phenomenon. The World Bistro & Gardens provides a memorable, albeit crowded, experience with a hidden grotto entrance that opens to a sprawling restaurant. Growler fills and merchandise are available in the gift shop, which has a decidedly more "corporate" feel than one might expect from this iconoclastic brewery. But visiting is a rite of passage for craft-beer fans—a touchstone experience. **1999 Citracado Pkwy., Escondido | stonebrewing.com**

LOST ABBEY/PORT BREWING CO.: If the crowd at Stone Brewing scares you off (or if you failed to make reservations at the restaurant and face a 3-hour wait for a table), the tasting room at Lost Abbey is only a couple of miles down the road. With Lost Abbey dedicated to Belgian-styles, sours, and the like and the Port brand focusing heavily on hoppy styles, most beer fans will find something to rave about. Worship in their chapel of *Brettanomyces* in San Marcos, or enjoy the more intimate experience at their Confessional in Cardiff. **155 Mata Wy., #104, San Marcos | lostabbey.com/locations/tasting-room / 2007 San Elijo Ave., Cardiff | lostabbey.com/locations/the-confessional**

RIP CURRENT BREWING: The brewery was named Very Small Brewing Company and Brewer of the Year at the 2015 Great American Beer Festival. Enjoy one of their highly rated IPAs (such as Lupulin Lust) or go for something darker, such as their Vanilla Storm imperial porter. **1325 Grand Ave., #100, San Marcos | ripcurrentbrewing.com**

BAGBY BEER COMPANY: Jeff Bagby earned his cred at a number of other San Diego breweries before opening his own spot in Oceanside. Today, it's a huge modern beer garden with a truly surprising number of both their own beers and guest taps (18 of their own, 35 guest taps), and if you can't find something on that tap list you love, you're not trying hard enough. **601 S. Coast Hwy., Oceanside | bagbybeer.com**

GOLDEN COAST MEAD: (below) They create three levels of mead: entry-level, which are light, refreshing, and honey-forward; longer-fermentation meads with fuller body and higher ABV, made with varietal honey; and an upcoming level that will be made from honey harvested right at Golden Coast that will provide a sense of place. They use ale yeast, California honeys, and add interesting ingredients such as oak or *Lactobacillus* to balance. Two tasting rooms are available: one in Oceanside, and the other in Julian. While they don't serve food, you can bring your own. **4089 Oceanside Blvd., Ste. H, Oceanside / 4470 Julian Rd., Julian | goldencoastmead.com**

ABNORMAL BEER CO.: Beer, wine, and food all combine at Abnormal into a singular experience. With very creative cuisine and a fantastic beer program (try the stouts, you won't regret it), it's the kind of place you might go for one round and end up spending the remainder of the night. **16990 Via Tazon, San Diego | abnormalbeer.co/**

TOOLBOX BREWING COMPANY: The preponderance of hops in San Diego county is no accident—this is the county that defined and honed the West Coast IPA style after all. So Toolbox is a bit of an outlier with their primary focus on sour and wild ales. The location is a bit out of the way, off in an office park that's otherwise pretty empty on the weekends, but the beer is expansive with a dozen or more riffs on sour and wild styles, from straightforward Berliner Weisses to mixed-fermentation fruit sours. **1495 Poinsettia Ave., #148, Vista | toolboxbrewing.com**

ALPINE

ALPINE BEER CO.: The fundamental question every beer traveler visiting San Diego must answer is whether to trek out to Alpine Beer, located roughly 45 minutes east of downtown San Diego in the town of Alpine. But let us make the answer easy for you—yes, go. On our visit, a line out the door had already formed just after their noon opening, and some of our queued compatriots made the 90-mile drive down from Orange County every month to restock on Pure Hoppiness double IPA, Duet IPA, and more. Grab lunch and a flight of samplers from their pub on the far side of the building, then hit the tap room for bottles and growlers to go. It's worth the drive and worth the wait. **2363 Alpine Blvd., Alpine | alpinebeerco.com**

TEMECULA

REFUGE BREWERY: If you find yourself out in Temecula, swing by the tap room and grab a pint of Blood Orange Wit or Grapefruit IPA. **43040 Rancho Wy., Temecula | refugebrew.com**

SAN CLEMENTE

PIZZA PORT SAN CLEMENTE: At the southern tip of Orange County is the northernmost outpost of the famed Pizza Port chain of brewpubs. This is the spot to stop for a pie and a couple of growlers on your way to or from beer nirvana in San Diego. **301 N. El Camino Real, San Clemente | pizzaport.com/locations/pizza-port-san-clemente**

LEFT COAST BREWING COMPANY: Oh, that Trestles IPA. *Craft Beer & Brewing Magazine*® scored it a 97—no small feat in a very crowded category. But their Voodoo Stout is no slouch either, earning a 95. Hit the tap room in San Clemente for non-packaged specials and one-off test batches. **1245 Puerta Del Sol, San Clemente | leftcoastbrewing.com**

ANAHEIM AND ORANGE COUNTY

THE BRUERY: This is easily the most well-known O.C. craft destination, and the bustling tasting room in Placentia is a must-visit for traveling beer lovers. The popular brewery opened a second tasting room dedicated to their Terreux (sour and funky beers) brand. You owe it yourself to order a barrel-aged or sour beer from their extensive menu because there's almost always one on. And always check their tasting room social media feed when planning your trip—at certain times of the year, you just might get lucky and find extra bottles of Black Tuesday on sale! But despite their penchant for big-barrelled beers, our favorite is still their hoppy Humulus Lager. **The Bruery: 717 Dunn Way, Placentia I thebruery.com / The Bruery Terreux: 1174 N. Grove St., Anaheim I brueryterreux.com**

NOBLE ALE WORKS: A local favorite known for their unbridled creativity, hops-bomb IPAs, and the Naughty Sauce (a golden coffee stout served on nitro that became a local phenomenon in 2014). **1621 S. Sinclair St., Anaheim I noblealeworks.com**

BOTTLE LOGIC BREWING: Another marquee Anaheim brewery that's garnering beer-geek accolades and plenty of trade board ISO posts. A couple of flights at the tasting room will show you what all the fuss is about. **1072 N. Armando St., Anaheim I bottlelogic.com**

LOS ANGELES

While craft beer flourished for decades just a hundred miles south in San Diego, until the current decade, Los Angeles remained a craft-beer desert of cocktails and mass-market brews. Then came the recession of 2008, and in a plot line familiar to those who follow craft beer, some of the intrepid homebrewers who were pushed out of the mainstream economy applied their DIY spirit to a new wave of brewery launches in Los Angeles. It didn't take long before the ever-thirsty populace began to take pride in its city's nascent craft-beer scene, and the region now sports more than three dozen breweries scattered throughout its infamous sprawl.

Los Angeles County comprises 88 cities spread across almost 5,000 square miles—calling it a sprawl hardly does justice to the incredible patchwork of municipalities, neighborhoods, freeways, and hidden gems. The size has been one of the biggest obstacles to the development of L.A.'s beer culture, but as the scene has developed, three particular areas have become home to clusters of breweries, and there are enough other notable hot spots scattered between them to keep a dedicated beer tourist busy for days.

THE SOUTH BAY AND LONG BEACH

Stretching along the coast from the LAX airport almost to the Orange County line, the South Bay is the shining beacon of craft beer in the Southland.

STRAND BREWING: It was the first brewery to open in South Bay, and it quickly became a favorite with the laid-back beach community. In 2015, Strand expanded into a larger production facility with an expanded tasting room to meet demand. **2201 Dominguez St., Torrance I strandbrewing.com**

SMOG CITY BREWERY: Smog City is perhaps the most talked about of the Torrance breweries, and with good reason—it does everything from drinkable Pilsners to fruited saisons to decadent barrel-aged treats, and it's all excellent.
1901 Del Amo Blvd., Torrance | smogcitybrewing.com

MONKISH BREWING: Just a block away from Smog City is Monkish Brewing—a small operation that emphasizes the flavors of fermentation with a range of Belgian-inspired farmhouse ales that creatively use uncommon ingredients (such as Asian teas or pistachio nuts). **20311 S. Western Ave., Torrance | monkishbrewing.com**

PHANTOM CARRIAGE BREWERY: (below) Part brewery, part beer bar, part barrel house, and part haunted mansion, it drips with spooky atmosphere and serves frighteningly good wild ales. It's the spot to grab a fortifying snack and a few tasters during a long day of beer exploration. **18525 S. Main St., Carson | phantomcarriage.com**

THE DUDES BREWING COMPANY: If you've enjoyed their canned options, swing by the Torrance tap room for 17 taps of mainline and special brews from their 3.5-barrel pilot system. **1840 W. 208th St., Torrance | thedudesbrew.com**

BROUWERIJ WEST: The indoor beer garden at the Port of L.A. in San Pedro is massive, and having seen the raw space in 2014 before construction began, we're even more impressed seeing the finished brewery and tasting room. The Belgian-inspired beers are tasty, and brewing geeks will enjoy seeing all the equipment up close, including the mash mixer they use to achieve very high efficiency. Kids and dogs are welcome. **110 E. 22nd St., San Pedro | brouwerijwest.com**

BEACHWOOD BBQ AND BREWING: (above) Beachwood gained national attention, twice winning Brewpub of the Year at the Great American Beer Festival. The grub is California-influenced barbeque, and the house beers are some of the best brews in Los Angeles. Brewmaster and Co-owner Julian Shrago is renowned for his punchy hops-bombs, but his skill at brewing subtle Old World styles is equally impressive. Don't be swayed by the always incredible list of guest taps and don't be fooled by the irreverent names of the beers (Tart Simpson Berliner Weisse, Udder Love milk stout)—Beachwood makes some of L.A.'s best beer. **210 E. 3rd St., Long Beach | beachwoodbbq.com**

THE L.A. BEACHES

NAJA'S PLACE: Among the moored boats and seafood eateries along the Redondo Beach International Boardwalk is one of the best seaside beer bars in the country. This L.A. institution has more than 70 taps (with an emphasis on IPAs) and a crowd as colorful as the tap handles covering the ceiling. **154 International Boardwalk, Redondo Beach | najasplace.com**

KING HARBOR BREWING: Just a few steps down the Redondo Beach International Boardwalk is the cozy Waterfront Tasting Room of Redondo's King Harbor Brewery, where you can enjoy some beer made for the beach (and take a crowler—32-oz can growler—to go). **132 International Boardwalk, Redondo Beach | kingharborbrewing.com**

SELECT BEER STORE: If you need some bottles for the hotel room or Airbnb, stop in at Redondo Beach's combination bottle shop and bar. **1613 S . Pacific Coast Hwy., Redondo Beach | selectbeerstore.com**

EL SEGUNDO BREWING: (right) From wet-hopped beers to the freshest possible bottles offered to drinkers to the unquenchable desire to keep refining and keep showing drinkers a new side of hoppy beers, El Segundo Brewing has become L.A.'s premier IPA brewery. With more than two-dozen IPAs in their lineup, there's no doubt this is the IPA-lover's mecca—even pro wrestler "Stone Cold" Steve Austin has a signature brew created just for his palate on tap. For those who want to go beyond an IPA, you can find a red, vanilla stout, passion fruit white dog, Berliner Weisse, and a few others. While they don't have an on-site kitchen, they frequently host food trucks and caterers. **140 Main St., El Segundo | elsegundobrewing.com**

FIRESTONE WALKER THE PROPAGATOR: This L.A.-area outpost for Firestone Walker brings their tap room exclusives, wild ales, and barrel-aged beauties to a bigger audience. Grab a bite from the kitchen (it's excellent) and an Unfiltered DBA, and enjoy. **3205 W. Washington Blvd., Marina Del Rey | firestonebeer.com/visit/venice.php**

LIBRARY ALE HOUSE: If you're on the west side, this is where to go for chef-driven bites and the brews to pair with them. **2911 Main St., Santa Monica | libraryalehouse.com**

HONORABLE MENTION: Anyone who's traveled through LAX knows just how crucial beer is to one's continued sanity. Fortunately, venues throughout Terminals 2, 6, 7, and the International Terminal pour Point the Way IPA and Get Up Offa That Brown from LA's own Golden Road Brewing (goldenroad.la).

NORTHEAST L.A.

Another early bastion of craft brewing in Los Angeles arose among the hip communities in the hills between Downtown and Pasadena. Some of L.A.'s biggest and best beer destinations are now found in these neighborhoods.

EAGLE ROCK BREWERY: It was the first production brewery to open within city limits of Los Angeles in decades, and the small tap room in the Glassell Park neighborhood is a favorite hangout and beer-tour stop. In 2014, the team opened the Eagle Rock Brewery Public House restaurant not far from the brewery, and the kitchen turns out some fantastic upscale beer cuisine to complement the brewery's refined portfolio. (They also serve one of the best

beer brunches in L.A.) **Brewery: 3056 Roswell St., Los Angeles | eaglerockbrewery .com / Public House: 1627 Colorado Blvd., Los Angeles | eaglerockpublichouse.com**

GOLDEN ROAD BREWING: Bordering the wild enclave of Griffith Park is L.A.'s biggest craft producer. Cans of Golden Road's drinkable Point the Way IPA and citrus-tinged Hefe are ubiquitous around town, and the pub's patio is a popular spot to relax with a pint (or pitcher)—especially for families. **5410 W. San Fernando Rd., Los Angeles | goldenroad.la**

MOHAWK BEND: This is the sister restaurant to Golden Road, and the destination gastropub in Echo Park offers 72 taps of brewed-in-California beers alongside a vegetarian- and vegan-friendly menu (don't pass up the Buffalo-style fried cauliflower). **2141 Sunset Blvd., Los Angeles | mohawk.la**

SUNSET BEER CO.: On Sunset Boulevard, the bar/bottle shop hybrid stocks an incredible selection, has a lounge, and is walking distance to Dodger Stadium if you want to catch a game. **1498 Sunset Blvd., Los Angeles | sunsetbeerco.com**

HIGHLAND PARK

Highland Park might be a bit of a journey from the core of Los Angeles, but it's one that any serious beer lover should make. The neighborhood has enough cafés, bars, shops, and taco trucks to fill out a leisurely day of walking and imbibing, and the neighborhood brewery is the main attraction.

HIGHLAND PARK BREWERY: Highland occupies a tiny space in back of The Hermosillo on York Boulevard. The once seedy dive has transformed into a lively wine and beer bar with a great menu and some incredible house beers. Brewer Bob Kunz is equally adept at the clean, hoppy ales that the locals demand and the funky, uncontrollable mixed-fermentation brews that he loves. **5127 York Blvd., Los Angeles | hpb.la**

MAXIMILIANO: Also on York Boulevard, you'll find this laid-back pizza and pasta restaurant, which has become the unofficial tasting room for Pasadena's Craftsman Brewery (craftsmanbrewing.com)—the oldest production brewery in the region. **5930 York Blvd., Los Angeles | maximilianohp.com**

DOWNTOWN L.A.

The transformed downtown core of Los Angeles bustles with renewed commerce, and craft beer has taken root again. The Arts District neighborhood just west of the L.A. River is the epicenter.

ANGEL CITY BREWERY: This is an ambitious project from Boston Beer–backed Alchemy and Science that pours a broad and creative lineup in their striking Art Deco tap room/art gallery/performance space. **216 Alameda St., Los Angeles | angelcitybrewery.com**

MUMFORD BREWING: (right) In 2015, they opened in The Arts District neighborhood. Their Great Uncle George barrel-aged Russian imperial stout and Mindclouder DIPA are highly rated, and they offer curbside pickup: if you order ahead, they will fill a growler and bring it out to your car. **416 Boyd St., Los Angeles | mumfordbrewing.com**

BOOMTOWN BREWERY: In 2014, Boomtown Brewery opened in The Arts District neighborhood. **700 Jackson St., Los Angeles | boomtownbrew.com**

ARTS DISTRICT BREWING: They opened in The Arts District neighborhood in December 2015 headed by Devon Randall from the legendary Pizza Port Solana Beach brewpub. They opened with 9 original beers including golden ales, stouts, and IPAs. The brewpub includes 10 restored vintage Skeeball machines. **828 Traction Ave., Los Angeles | 213dthospitality.com/project/arts-district-brewing-co**

LITTLE TOKYO FAR BAR: Little Tokyo boasts an impressive selection of imported Japanese craft beers in bottles and 34 taps with Japanese and local favorites, including Firestone Walker Stickee Monkee and The Bruery Mischief. **347 E. 1st St., Los Angeles | farbarla.com**

THE SPRAWL

Beyond the notable clusters of craft-beer activity in Los Angeles are many other shining stars scattered among the grit, glitz, freeways, and neighborhoods of Los Angeles.

BLUE PALMS BREWHOUSE: Just steps off the Walk of Fame is this superlative beer bar with 24 taps, a stellar bottle list., and some of the best pub food in the city. **6124 Hollywood Blvd., Los Angeles | bluepalmsbrewhouse.com**

VERDUGO BAR: The dim interior with regular DJs offers a more active experience, but the casual patio filled with brewery ephemera and rotating food trucks is a more chill way to enjoy their killer beer offerings. **3408 Verdugo Rd., Los Angeles | verdugobar.com**

THREE WEAVERS BREWING COMPANY: Their imperial red, Blood Junkie, took home gold at World Beer Cup 2016, and the cool, open, industrial tap room and brewery are tempered by their dedication to community first. Brewmaster Alexandra Nowell brewed for a number of well-known breweries before landing at Three Weavers, and you can taste the discipline and creativity in every glass. **1031 W. Manchester Blvd., Inglewood | threeweavers.la**

BEER BELLY: Known for its madcap take on comfort food and a tightly curated 12-tap beer list. **532 S. Western Ave., Los Angeles | beerbellyla.com**

FATHER'S OFFICE: The nationally acclaimed establishment by Chef Sang Yoon in Culver City features chef-driven bites and 36 rotating craft-beer taps to pair with them. **3229 Helms Ave., Los Angeles | fathersoffice.com**

SAN FERNANDO VALLEY

MACLEOD'S ALE COMPANY: A young brewery that focuses on traditional British styles and serves all their beer hand-pumped from casks. Classic, flavorful brews—Macleod's keeps it real (in more ways than one) and proves that traditional beer can be relevant in unconventional ways. **14741 Calvert St., Van Nuys | macleodale.com**

LADYFACE ALE COMPANIE: Fancy a hike? Head into the hills that rise above Malibu and enjoy a post-trail meal here. It's not your average brewpub, and the food is as excellent as the (often Belgian-style) beer. **29281 Agoura Rd., Agoura Hills | ladyfaceale.com**

CENTRAL COAST

FIRESTONE WALKER BREWERY: There are few experiences in the world of craft beer like a visit to the Firestone Walker brewery and restaurant. Everything they do, they do to the absolute best of their ability—whether that's technical brewing, restaurant hospitality, the design of the tour experience, barrel-aging big beers, or Brewmaster Matt Brynildson's exceptionally masterful nose for hops. The brewery itself is built around a self-guided walking tour for guests who want to do it themselves, or sign up for a guided tour and get an in-depth look at their precise and impeccably designed brewing systems. You can find their limited-release barrel-aged beers on sale in the gift shop and tap room/restaurant, but for the full experience save time for a meal—their kitchen is fantastic. For a hospitality experience on steroids, buy tickets for their annual Firestone Walker Invitational Beer Festival— tickets typically sell out in less than a minute as eager fans flock to what is one of the best beer festivals in the world! **1400 Ramada Dr., Paso Robles, l firestonebeer.com/**

FIRESTONE WALKER BARRELWORKS: Many brewers keep their sour-beer brewing operations separate from their "clean" beer, but for most that means a wall or another warehouse full of sour barrels. For Firestone Walker, that means a separate facility 90 miles south of the brewery in Buellton where wort is trucked in, pumped into barrels, and aged on sour and funky cultures. The design, which looks a bit like a medieval church on the inside, references the reverence they take with these beers. And the attached tasting room is a shrine to which any acolyte should make a pilgrammage. **620 McMurray Rd., Buellton l firestonebeer.com/visit/buellton.php**

FIGUEROA MOUNTAIN BREWING CO: Thirteen GABF medals and 3 World Beer Cup medals over the past 6 years are evidence of the brewing talent at Figueroa Mountain Brewing, and their six locations—three of which include restaurants—have expanded throughout the central coast and valley to slake the thirst of craft beer fans. If it's on tap, you must order "I Dunkeled In My Pants," for obvious reasons. **45 Industrial Wy., Buellton / 137 Anacapa St., Ste F, Santa Barbara / 2446 Alamo Pintado Ave,, Los Olivos / 30770 Russell Ranch Rd., Stes E & F, Westlake Village / 560 E. Betteravia, Ste. B, Santa Maria / 1462 E. Grand Ave., Arroyo Grande l figmtnbrew.com/taprooms**

THE LIBERTINE BREWING COMPANY: (below left) Now with two locations (the original Morro Bay pub and the newer brewery in San Luis Obispo), The Libertine is the brainchild of charismatic brewer Tyler Clark and focuses solely on brewing wild and sour beers. They're one of the few breweries that still uses the process of stein brewing (the process of using superheated rocks instead of steam or direct fire) to heat the wort. And instead of using cultured, pitched yeast, they draw everything from the environment around them—dust in the rafters carries lots of *Lactobacillus* and *Brettanomyces,* as well as other microorganisms—to produce their sour wild ales. Even some of their hops are harvested onsite. Oak barrels hold their lineup of beers that are often aged for a year or more on fruit and other ingredients. The new brewery in SLO has allowed them to significantly expand their brewing operation, so look for their bottles at better shops around California, as well. **801 Embarcadero, Morro Bay / 1234 Broad St, San Luis Obispo l libertinebrewing.com**

CASA AGRIA SPECIALTY ALES: The central California wild and sour beer scene continues to heat up, as newcomer Casa Agria brings the funk to Oxnard. Hype aside, it's fantastic to see farmhouse beers made with local produce in a part of the country that grows so much fruit. And if sour beer isn't your thing, they still offer a couple hoppy options as well. **701 N. Del Norte Blvd., #310, Oxnard l casaagria.com**

SOUTHERN CENTRAL VALLEY

DIONYSUS BREWING: The idea of a sour beer brewer in Bakersfield caught us by surprise, but their membership program lets them ship anywhere in California, making the idea not quite so crazy. The tap room isn't just sour beer—stouts, blonde ales, IPAs, and cream ales make regular appearances—but their sour beers are definitely the stars of the show. **6201 Schirra Ct., #13, Bakersfield | dionysusbrewing.com**

KERN RIVER BREWING COMPANY: The country branding theme might have you thinking that they're traditionalists, but one taste of their Citra DIPA will have you thinking differently. Bright, clear, punchy, unadulterated hops love. And if hops aren't your thing, the Sequoia Red and Class V Stout will not let you down. **13415 Sierra Wy., Kernville | kernriverbrewing.com**

DUSTBOWL BREWING: Brewmaster Don Oliver turned a win in the Samuel Adams LongShot homebrew competition into a full time gig, and business has been so strong lately that they had to build a new brewery to handle it. Stop in for 14 beers on tap, and if hops are your thing, don't miss the Therapist triple IPA. **3000 Fulkerth Rd., Turlock | dustbowlbrewing.com**

SANTA CRUZ AND CAPITOLA

SANTE ADAIRIUS RUSTIC ALES: Located in the coastal city of Capitola, in a glorified warehouse with a cozy tasting room, Sante Adiarius draws its inspiration from traditional Belgian beers and brewing methods. Saisons represent an ancient approach to thinking about beer—using ingredients that are local and seasonal, working with what you have—which is why Sante Adairius specializes in the style. If it's available, grab a glass of the steel-fermented Saison Bernice, bottles of the wood-fermented Cellarman, their fruited saisons such as West Ashley (with apricots) or Appreciation (blackberries), and taste the spectrum of flavors in their farmhouse-style beers. Their barrel-aged beers don't have a huge emphasis on wine or oak character, but are more focused on keeping the mixed cultures active and alive, adding depth of flavor and roundness to the beers. And don't stop there—world-class IPAs, pale ales, and porters round out their lineup and offer plenty of options for those who are less saison-inclined. No food is served on premises, but you can order in or bring your own. **103 Kennedy Dr., Capitola | rusticales.com**

LÚPULO CRAFT BEER HOUSE: We first ran into Stuyvie, the co-owner of Lupulo, while he was picking up kegs at The Rare Barrel (a 2-hour drive in traffic from his bar in Santa Cruz). This kind of long distance dedication to bringing in the best beer possible, even with breweries who don't work through distributors, is what sets Lupulo apart. As a result, you'll find breweries such as the aforemention Rare Barrel, Berkeley's Fieldwork, San Francisco's Cellarmaker, and others, flowing regularly. On top of that, they regularly feature a couple taps from local friends Sante Adairius. The menu of light sandwiches and tapas is tasty, but feel free to politely decline when the bartender offers Underberg bitters later in the evening. **233 Cathcart St., Santa Cruz | lupulosc.com**

SAN FRANCISCO

ALMANAC BEER COMPANY: Featuring an impressive lineup of barrel-aged and blended beers, Almanac houses 1,700 oak barrels and counting, many of which are sours. In addition to the barrel-aged offerings, Almanac's beers include a gose, a saison, and an IPA. They harvested yeast cultures from bottles left over from bottle parties, as well as commercial bugs, to create their house flavor. Even more flavor comes from the barrels, with additional elements of wine, oak, and vanilla. While they don't have a tasting room or offer tours, you can check the Events page on their website for special tasting events throughout the state (and beyond!).
2325 3rd St., #222, San Francisco | almanacbeer.com

CITY BEER STORE: A friendly watering hole where you can sip the beer while browsing the shelves for your next great find. The beer geek staff is happy to help customers choose from their alluring brews. The prices on hard-to-find bottles (such as Cantillon) are high, but that's the reason they might still be in stock when you visit, so if you're in the mood to splurge on some great bottles, City Beer is the place to do it. **1168 Folsom St., #101, San Francisco | citybeerstore.com**

THE MONK'S KETTLE: Located in the funky Mission District, The Monk's Kettle is a high-end beer bar with an emphasis on beer-friendly cuisine. The staff has a reputation for putting only the best on their list of 28 taps and their massive bottle menu. **3141 16th St., San Francisco | monkskettle.com**

CELLARMAKER BREWING COMPANY: This is one of the most cellar-focused craft breweries in San Francisco, if not the country, and accordingly named. From their geography-defying take on hazy IPAs and pales to an unwavering focus on freshness, they've built a reputation as a Bay Area institution in less than 3 years. Their rotating lineup consists of some meticulously crafted IPAs and pale ales, as well as the occasional blonde ale, smoked coffee porter, saison, rye English bitter, barrel-aged selections, and kettle-soured beer. There's no kitchen on site, but you can bring your own or order from one of the nearby local restaurants who deliver. Only patrons 21 and over are allowed in the brewery. **1150 Howard St., San Francisco | cellarmakerbrewing.com**

TORONADO: The music is loud, the service can be gruff, and the bathrooms are graffiti masterpieces…but it's all part of the charm at Toronado. With more than 40 taps, some flown in just for special events, reading their draught list is like reading a Who's Who of beer. **547 Haight St., San Francisco | toronado.com**

MAGNOLIA GASTROPUB & BREWERY: Located at hippie ground zero, on Haight Street, Magnolia Gastropub & Brewery has been serving traditional bitters and milds (for which Founder Dave McLean has always had a deep love) alongside American styles and cask ales for more than 17 years. Uber chill vibes pervade throughout the pub; there's a good chance some Grateful Dead tunes will come through the speakers; and the Slow Food-inspired menu features hearty, well-done fare. **1398 Haight St., San Francisco | magnoliapub.com**

MIKKELLER BAR: Gorgeous and modern, exquisite but pricey draft list, mildly gruff and impersonal service—Mikkel Borg Bjergsø's Mikkeller

Bar is geared toward professionals not tourists, and a certain amount of knowledge is key to an enjoyable visit. But for those who aren't put off by this barrier to entry, it offers a fanatically curated tap list and beer served and presented impeccably well. **34 Mason St., San Francisco | mikkellerbar.com**

ANCHOR BREWING: (above) When Fritz Maytag bought the brewery back in the 1960s, he had no way of knowing just how fundamental it would be in the rebirth of the flavorful beer we now call "craft." But under his guidance, the brewery went from "struggling" to a worldwide influencer and pioneer. Today, that history is front and center at the brewery, from the copper-clad brewhouse to the vintage wood-paneled bar. **1705 Mariposa St., San Francisco | anchorbrewing.com**

HOPWATER DISTRIBUTION: Thirty taps of expertly selected all California beer, a gorgeous interior, and upscale pub fare makes Hopwater a great stop in Nob Hill. **850 Bush St., San Francisco | hopwaterdistribution.com**

THE BEER HALL: San Francisco's got style, and this 24-tap outpost in mid Market is an attractive spot for enjoying beautiful beers. The ever-rotating draft and bottle lineup focuses on the best California has to offer, with special appearances from similarly cool breweries around the country and across the globe. **1 Polk St., San Francisco | thebeerhallsf.com**

HONORABLE MENTION: Speakeasy Ales & Lagers (goodbeer.com) is in a tougher part of town (rent on a production-sized facility in San Francisco isn't cheap), but their brand-inspired tasting room offers a fun place to try their well-made beers; Zeitgeist (zeitgeistsf.com) has the Mission covered with its craft-beer dive-bar aesthetic and hipster clientele; La Trappe (latrappecafe.com) goes deep on Belgian beer and pairs with a classic menu of Belgian food.

EAST BAY

THE RARE BARREL: (right) Establishing itself as one of the leading sour beer breweries in the country, The Rare Barrel experiments with an assortment of souring processes, ingredients, and implements. Each beer is brewed using one of three base recipes (golden ale, red ale, and dark ale) then aged for 3 to 6 months before the team tastes it and decides what fruits, spices, or other additions might work best with the base flavors. Some signature additions include ginger, rose hips, apricots, orange peel, elderberries, lavender, sour cherries, and vanilla beans. Head over to the tasting room, where you can sample 5–10 beers on tap, bottles from the cellar, buy a bottle to go, or sample one of their non-sour guest wines or beers. **940 Parker St., Berkeley | therarebarrel.com**

THE TRAPPIST & TRAPPIST PROVISIONS: Classic and new-school Belgian and Belgian-style beers sit side by side with beers from some of the best craft brewers across the country. Light fare such as cheese and meat trays are available to accompany the world-class beer lineup, but the beer is the star of the show at both locations. If you're lucky (like we were on our last visit), you might just stumble across bottles of Drie Fonteinen Hommage or Intense Red in the cooler or shelves. **The Trappist: 460 8th St., Oakland / Provisions: 6309 College Ave., Oakland | thetrappist.com**

BEER REVOLUTION: The small but potent tap room is home to around 50 taps and just enough Berkeley-style counterculture attitude to make it fun. Like most great beer bars, the tap list is about half locals, a quarter from around the state, and another quarter from the rest of the country and globe—the perfect way to try beers from a lot of great breweries without the increased carbon footprint from driving there. **464 3rd St., Oakland | beer-revolution.com**

TRIPLE ROCK BREWERY & ALEHOUSE: One of the oldest extant brewpubs in America, Triple Rock helped kick start the craft-beer craze back in the 1980s and has survived and thrived while others have moved on. **1920 Shattuck Ave., Berkeley | triplerock.com**

FIELDWORK BREWING: Their simple and elegant aesthetic carries through in the beer, with honest and creative hops riffs as well as a few farmhouse ales and stouts for good measure. **1160 Sixth St., Berkeley | fieldworkbrewing.com**

SIERRA NEVADA TORPEDO ROOM: If you can't make the trip all the way to Chico, this Berkeley outpost of the legendary brewery offers a quicker fix with tap room exclusives, rare releases, and some education thrown in for good measure. **2031 Fourth St., Berkeley | sierranevada.com**

DRAKE'S BREWING BARREL HOUSE: Aromacoma, Denogginizer, Hopocalypse—hard to go wrong with anything in Drake's hoppy ouevre. The Barrel House tap room (on the edge of a shopping center in San Leandro right next to the brewhouse), is tucked into a corner and a bit hard to find, but those who visit are rewarded with unpretentious, delicious beers. If you can't get down to San Leandro, their Drake's Dealership location in downtown Oakland offers the same great beer in a friendly rustic urban beer garden location. **Barrel House: 1933 Davis St., #177, San Leandro / Dealership: 2325 Broadway, Oakland | drinkdrakes.com**

21ST AMENDMENT BREWERY: This huge former Kelloggs cereal plant now turns different grains into gold under the command of the brewers

that implore us to Brew Free Or Die. They have huge plans for the San Leandro tasting room, but for now it's a fantastic place to gawk at their massive gleaming brewhouse and sip on favorites such as Hell Or High Watermelon.
2010 Williams St., San Leandro | 21st-amendment.com

HOP GRENADE: Brought to you by the folks behind The Brewing Network, this Concord beer bar and bottle shop is beautifully appointed, thoughtfully curated and imminently comfortable for a pint or two or four. **2151 Salvio St., Concord | thehopgrenade.com**

WINE COUNTRY

HERETIC BREWING COMPANY: Accomplished homebrewing author Jamil Zainasheff's commercial brewery is worth a stop for their focus on creative, boundary-pushing experimentation. **1052 Horizon Dr., Fairfield | hereticbrewing.com**

MOYLAN'S BREWERY: The classic Irish pub meets creative craft brewery at Moylans. Try the exquisitely simple Dragoons Dry Irish Stout, or if you like hops by the bale-full, order a Hopsickle DIPA or Hop Craic quadruple IPA. **15 Rowland Wy., Novato | moylans.com**

LAGUNITAS PETALUMA TAPROOM: Founder Tony Magee has plenty of stories to tell about this storied brewery location, but visitors are advised to get there early and get ready to wait—demand for tables outpaces the supply on weekends. If you order from the bar, make sure that your entire party (and all of their IDs) are there with you—they don't take the threat of undercover shutdown lightly and aren't taking any chances. But once you're past that bit of paranoia, you'll find interesting pilot brews, one-off takes on Lagunitas classics, and comfortable grounds to hang out on while enjoying their beer as fresh as it gets. **1280 N. McDowell Blvd., Petaluma | lagunitas.com/taprooms/petaluma**

RUSSIAN RIVER BREWING CO: For most craft-beer fans, Russian River needs no introduction. This is the home of Pliny, for crying out loud. But in case you really don't know, let's make it very clear—if you are within a 100-mile radius of this brewery, you owe it to yourself to visit. Whether you're looking for fresh Pliny the Elder (Double IPA), lining up in February for Pliny the Younger (the Triple IPA version), nursing one of brewmaster Vinnie Cilurzo's American sour beers such as Consecration or Supplication, or sticking with their clean and crisp STS Pils, there is literally no way to have a bad beer experience at the Russian River brewpub. If crowds aren't your thing, go on an off night—we showed up on a Saturday, once, and waited in a 50+ person line to get a table. But once seated, with a beer in hand, we had no complaints whatsoever. **725 4th St., Santa Rosa | russianriverbrewing.com**

MOONLIGHT BREWING: We first experienced Moonlight while drinking at Toronado in San Francisco—the English-style IPA was a stark contrast to the other hoppy beers on the menu, and expertly crafted. At press time, the tap room is only open Fri–Sun, but with a major investment from Lagunitas, we expect a bit of expansion and more access to Brewer Brian Hunt's great beers. **3350, Coffey Ln., Ste. A, Santa Rosa | moonlightbrewing.com**

BEAR REPUBLIC BREWING COMPANY: Fresh Racer 5 IPA in low key tap room that's equal parts diner and dive bar. Sign us up. **345 Healdsburg Ave., Healdsburg | bearrepublic.com**

ANDERSON VALLEY BREWING CO: Forgive their questionable approach to phonetic spelling, apparently it's a regional affectation (what exactly is "bahl hornin'" anyway?). Nonetheless, Anderson Valley has been making unique beers in their own little spaces for years (like that Wild Turkey barrel-aged beer series with a very different approach to barrel-aging than most). Today, their embrace of the gose style, and their willingness to can it, means new drinkers think of them more for their Blood Orange Gose than Barney Flats Oatmeal Stout. But no matter what your preference, AVBC is a great stop, and their approach to sustainability is great to see. **17700 Boonville Rd., Boonville | avbc.com**

NORTH COAST BREWING TAPROOM: When we think about seminal beers in certain styles, it's surprising how many of those beers have been brewed by North Coast. Old Rasputin, Brother Thelonius, Old Stock—so many genre-defining beers—and their tap room and grill in Fort Bragg is a fantastic place to experience them. **444 N. Main St., Fort Bragg | northcoast brewing.com/brewery-taproom/**

NORTHERN CENTRAL VALLEY

SIERRA NEVADA BREWING CO: They are quite possibly the most influential and important brewery in the history of craft beer, and a visit to the brewery in Chico is a pilgrimmage not to be taken lightly. Whether you're a brewer or a drinker, there is no way to walk away from a tour unimpressed—everything Sierra Nevada does is done thoughtfully, artfully, and

and with no expense spared. For the full experience, sign up for a tour—they offer a number of different tours focused on different aspects of the brewery such as hops and sustainability. And make sure you book in advance as they fill up quickly on busier weekends. If the guided tour isn't your thing, grab a seat in the brewpub and sample through the offerings from their pilot brewery—their small pilot system is as impressive as many smaller breweries' main brewhouses! **1075 East 20th St., Chico | sierranevada.com**

KNEE DEEP BREWING: With beer names such as Hoptologist, Lupulin River, Breaking Bud, and Midnight Hoppyness, it's pretty apparent where Knee Deep's interests lie. Grab a taster tray from the bar, sit at one of the indoor picnic tables overlooking the brewhouse floor, and watch the hops magicians at work. **13395 New Airport Rd., Auburn | kneedeepbrewing.com**

SUDWERK BREWING COMPANY: Finding a niche in craft beer is harder and harder these days, but the folks behind Sudwerk have gone deep on lagers and we've loved the results. From hoppy lagers to crisp traditional lagers and even sour beers, they're doing creative work with traditional techniques. Grab a glass, take a tour, feel the lager love. **2001 2nd St., Davis | sudwerkbrew.com**

MT. SHASTA

MT. SHASTA BREWING COMPANY: First creamery then brewery, Mt. Shasta Brewing Company is the perfect venue for soaking in the history of Mt. Shasta and some of its finest suds. Bikes adorn the ceiling of this funky bistro where hungry skiers and boarders can find cheese and meat boards, pizzas, bratwursts, and hot dogs. **360 College Ave., Weed | weedales.com**

MAMMOTH LAKE

MAMMOTH BREWING COMPANY: Ever had a lobster corn dog before? How about hops tater tots? Pair these with a Golden Trout Pilsner at Mammoth Brewing Company aprés-ski at Mammoth Mountain. **18 Lake Mary Rd., Mammoth Lakes | mammothbrewingco.com**

TRUCKEE AND LAKE TAHOE

FIFTYFIFTY BREWING: Nestled in the mountain town of Truckee, just down the road from Northstar at Tahoe resort, FiftyFifty is best known for their Eclipse barrel-aged imperial stout. But a stop at the brewpub will quickly show you just how good they are at brewing many other styles as well. The kitchen offers plenty of creative options, but the real reason to go is to sample the special barrel-aged beers that don't make it into wide distribution, such as B.A.R.T., Annularity, Old Conundrum, and more. **11197 Brockway Rd., #1, Truckee | fiftyfiftybrewing.com**

TAHOE MOUNTAIN BREWING CO. BREWPUB: Taste local barrel-aged, sour, and wild beers at Tahoe Mountain Brewing Co.'s Brewpub, a relatively new kid on the block (opened in 2012) in the epic ski town. The brewery's Apricot Recolte Du Bois won a 2014 GABF medal in the Wood-and-Barrel-Aged Sour Beer category. **475 N. Lake Blvd., Tahoe City | tahoebrewing.com/brewpub**

ALASKA

Alaska has some of the most intense weather and terrain of all the 50 states, but there's no reason to let that stop you from quenching your thirst at one of their breweries. While you're there, take in some of the gorgeous scenery while planning your adventures for the days to come. Alaska brewery laws allow patrons to consume 36 oz/person/day on premise, and purchase beer to go by the liter or half gallon growler.

BEST SPOTS FOR OLD SCHOOL BEER STYLES

49th State Brewing Co.'s beers are steeped in British, German, and U.S. tradition while King Street Brewing Company in Anchorage brews up some great traditional German-style beers.

BEST SPOTS FOR NEW SCHOOL BEER STYLES

Anchorage Brewing Company uses cool fermentation techniques in their specialty barrel-aged beers, creating a buzz that extends throughout the lower 48 and beyond. And their yearly Culmination festival brings the best of the rest of the world to Anchorage.

BEST SPOTS TO ENJOY A MEAL WITH YOUR BEER

Humpy's Great Alaskan Alehouse's high-end pub-style focuses on local seafood that pairs well with cream-of-the crop beers on draft or on their bottle list, and Chair 5 serves American fare and some incredible Alaskan specialties.

MOST STYLISH TAPROOMS AND BARS

49th State's Denali brewpub has an industrial/lodge look, with a massive circular fireplace in the center. Glacier Brewhouse's homey mountain cozy lodge interior is Alaska personified.

MOST AWARD-WINNING BREWERIES

Alaskan Brewing Co.'s beers have garnered a whopping 47 GABF medals plus another 19 from the World Beer Cup, while also earning high ratings from the CB&B blind-tasting review panels.

BEST UNIQUE BEER EXPERIENCE

Hangar on the Wharf offers 24 taps, 80+ beers in bottles and cans, and gorgeous views of mountains, water, cruise ships, and bi-planes taking off and landing.

ANCHORAGE

HUMPY'S GREAT ALASKAN ALEHOUSE: While Anchorage has a population that is only a little more than 300,000, the state draws almost two million visitors annually. Between the two, the thirst for great beer is high, and Humpy's 54 taps and a small—but respectable—bottle list present the best options for quenching it. The draft list is strong on Alaskan beers, and the beer buyers' discriminating palates do a stellar job of zeroing in on the cream of the crop. Be sure to check out local favorites King Street Brewing and Glacier Brewhouse. The real draw, though, is finding rare gems such as Midnight Sun's Sloth Belgian Imperial Stout or Anchorage Brewing Company one-offs gracing the beer-menu pages. The high-end pub-style fare focuses on local seafood (particularly Alaskan king crab), and part-owner Billy Opinsky has been known to pour vintage Cantillon and other whales from the stupid-deep cellar at their occasional beer dinners. **610 W. 6th Ave., Anchorage | humpysalaska.com**

ANCHORAGE BREWING COMPANY: The specialty at Anchorage is barrel fermentation, with some cool brews that feature *Brettanomyces* and other sour cultures. Among its most sought-after beers are the Galaxy IPA, a white IPA that's bottled with *Brett,* and Love Buzz, a saison that's fermented with *Brett* and has citrusy, floral notes. Bottles can be enjoyed in the tap room, and a select list is available to go. They also feature guest brewers from time to time. Food is served occasionally on site. There is an outdoor seating area where you can snuggle up in front of the fire pit while sipping and listening to a live music act. **148 W. 91st St., Anchorage | anchoragebrewingcompany.com**

MIDNIGHT SUN BREWING CO.: Upstairs from the main brewery is The Loft, the tasting room that serves up their own beer and offers a casual dining experience. They have a revolving tap featuring their year-round brews, as well as seasonals and specialties. A few to check out include the Berserker Imperial Stout, which has notes of whiskey, red wine, dark fruit, and tobacco; the Sockeye Red IPA, brewed with Centennial, Cascade, and Simcoe hops; and the Arctic Devil Barley Wine, aged in wine, port, or whiskey barrels. Food is served every day. **8111 Dimond Hook Dr., Anchorage | midnightsunbrewing.com**

GLACIER BREWHOUSE: Barrel lovers will want to make this a must-visit brewery—they have a "Wall of Wood" made up of 50 barrels made from various types of wood that have previously aged a variety of liquors and wines. The India Pale Ale is a clean and crisp beer that's been double dry hopped in both the aging tank and the serving tank. The Oatmeal Stout is a roasty brew with notes of chocolate. And the Bavarian Hefeweizen is an unfiltered wheat with notes of banana and clove. They rotate in a daily cask-conditioned ale. The food menu leans toward the upscale side with tons of Alaskan seafood and meats, and the lunch, dinner, and dessert menus each have a gluten-free version. **737 W. 5th Ave., #110, Anchorage | glacierbrewhouse.com**

BROKEN TOOTH BREWING: Both the Great American Beer Festival and World Beer Cup have lauded some of the brews coming out of Broken Tooth, formerly known as Moose's Tooth. Some of the award-winners include Darth Delirium, Smokin' Willie Porter, Prince William Porter, and Bear Tooth Ale. We also recommend the Fairweather IPA, YellowEye P.A., and L'enfant Terrible. Beers are available on tap, in growlers, and some in cans. **2021 Spar Ave., Anchorage | brokentoothbrewing.net**

BEAR TOOTH THEATREPUB & THE BEAR TOOTH GRILL: Owned by the same people as Broken Tooth Brewing, the theatrepub offers freshly prepared Southwestern food, and on draft is Broken Tooth Brewing and wine. The beer and wine is for enjoying inside the theater, while the grill offers food fresh off the grill as well as a full-service bar. They show a combination of new releases, classics, and documentaries. **1230 W. 27th Ave., Anchorage | beartooththeatre.net / beartoothgrill.net**

MOOSE'S TOOTH PUB & PIZZERIA: A third location in the Broken Tooth and Bear Tooth lineup is Moose's Tooth, which serves up gourmet stone-baked pizza, along with a variety of Broken Tooth Brewing's year-round, first-tap, and specialty beers. This location is also a large concert venue that features an impressive lineup of national acts. **3300 Old Seward Hwy., Anchorage | moosestooth.net**

49TH STATE ANCHORAGE: With a staff of Cicerone-certified beer servers and the right glassware to serve up each style of beer, you know you're in a beer-enthusiast's heaven. The Solstice IPA is citrusy, piney, and juicy; the Baked Blonde is unfiltered, with some fruity, floral, honey notes; and the McCarthy's Stout is a dry Irish stout with some roasty chocolaty goodness. Tours are available by reservation only and for a small fee. And if you're looking for something more lively to do, they feature live concerts, trivia nights, two theaters, and a rooftop patio. **717 W. 3rd Ave., Anchorage | 49statebrewing.com/anchorage**

KING ST. BREWING COMPANY: Cozy up with some friends in the small tasting room at King St. and try one of 6–8 rotating beers on tap. Some are available in cans, bottles, and growlers to go, too. The unfiltered Hefeweizen is full of flavor, with notes of banana and clove. The Pilsner is brewed in the Czech tradition, and is clean and crisp. In addition to the year-round and seasonal beers, they offer blends of some of their favorites. No food is on site, so if you're settling in for a bite you'll have to bring your own food. **7924 King St., Anchorage | kingstreetbrewing.com**

CHAIR 5 RESTAURANT: If you can get through the night by following a few key rules (no gunfights, fist fights, food fights, or cursing) you're all set to chill for a spot at Chair 5. Their extensive beer list has premium Alaskan brews, some from the Pacific Northwest, domestics, and a nice list of imports. Wine by the bottle or glass is available, as well as an exclusive Executive Wine List, single malt Scotch, Tequila. Food is American fare, with some impressive Alaskan specialties. **171 Lindblad Ave., Girdwood | chairfive.com**

KENAI & SOLDOTNA

KASSIK'S KENAI BREW STOP: You can find 10 beers on tap in this 7 BBL brewhouse, and despite its small size, Kassik has rounded up several medals at the World Beer Championship and World Beer Cup. Winning brews include Caribou Kilt, Big Nutz Imperial Brown, Barley Wine, and Smoked Russian Imperial Stout. We also recommend Morning Wood, Dolly Varden Nut Brown, and Beaver Tail Blonde. In addition to the taps, many of their brews can be taken home in bottles or growlers. **7160 Spruce Haven St., Kenai | kassiksbrew.com**

KENAI RIVER BREWING COMPANY: The lodge-style tap room has plenty of room to grab a seat and hang out for a while indoors, or if the weather's nice (or if you've brought kids, who are not allowed in the tasting room) sit outside on the patio. Eight to ten beers are usually on tap, and you can take cans, growlers, pigs, and kegs to go. There is no kitchen or onsite food, but some days they have a food truck/cart, or you can have it delivered. The Sunken Island IPA is an amber-hued beer with a nice blend of spicy hops and rich malt with a touch of yeast. The Skilak Scottish is a dark amber Scottish ale with a smooth malt profile and a smoky, roasty character. **308 Homestead Ln., Soldotna | kenairiverbrewing.com**

DENALI

DENALI BREWING COMPANY: The bright, homey tasting room is perfect for unwinding with friends, or head outside to the beer garden. Four signature beers are always on tap: Twister Creek IPA, Single Engine Red, Chuli Stout, and Mother Ale. Some of the more notable seasonals include Mother Superior and Flag Stop Mile Post 1. A food truck visits every weekend, but the brewery is also attached to Twister Creek Restaurant. **Mile 2 Talkeetna Spur Rd., Talkeetna | denalibrewing.com**

DENALI BREWING COMPANY AND BREWPUB: This is the sister to Denali Brewing Company, offering soups, salads, sandwiches, and some more unique dishes that feature Alaskan ingredients. Several of Denali Brewing's beers are on tap and may differ from what's at the tasting room. In addition to what's on tap you can grab six- and twelve-packs, growlers, specialty bottles, and kegs to go. **13605 E. Main St., Talkeetna | denalibrewing.com/brewpub**

49TH STATE BREWING CO. DENALI PARK BREWPUB: With a staff of Cicerone-certified beer serves and the right glassware to serve up each style of beer, you know you're in a beer-enthusiast's heaven. The Solstice IPA is citrusy, piney, and juicy; the Baked Blonde is unfiltered, with some fruity, floral, honey notes; and the McCarthy's Stout is a dry Irish stout with some roasty chocolaty goodness. Beer is also brewed at this location, so grab a pint at the beer garden then start up a game of disc golf, bocce ball, horseshoes, or bags. Live concerts are on the events schedule, as well as a variety of other events. **Mile 248.4 George Parks Hwy., Healy | 49statebrewing.com**

FAIRBANKS

SILVER GULCH BREWING & BOTTLING CO.: Located a few degrees south of the Arctic Circle, this brewery is the most northerly in the United States. A favorite of the locals, Silver Gulch includes a pub and a restaurant in addition to the brewery. Although rustic on the outside, its modern and cozy on the inside. Four beers are available year-round in bottles and on draft: Pick Axe Porter, Fairbanks Lager, Coldfoot Pilsner Lager, and Copper Creek Amber Ale. 50 States Stout, brewed in celebration of American Craft Beer Week 2016, is highly rated as is Osculum Infame, a spiced Belgian quad that is one of their specialty beers. **2195 Old Steese Hwy. N., Fox | silvergulch.com**

JUNEAU

ALASKAN BREWING CO.: We rated their Alaskan Stout a 93, White a 91, and Pumpkin Porter a 91, and they won a bronze at the Great American Beer Festival for their Smoked Porter. And in addition to their great beer, they're working hard to protect Alaska's environment—what's not to love? Other recommended beers include Amber, Freeride APA, and Icy Bay IPA. The tasting room offers a $5 tour, which offers some "beerducation" and 6 samples, as well as a souvenir. Beers on tap are rotating, featuring regular favorites, seasonals, and special brews. No food is allowed on site, so come with a full stomach. **5429 Shaune Dr., Juneau | alaskanbeer.com**

THE ALASKAN HOTEL BAR: This is a historic bar and hotel, and if you're up to get rowdy with the locals and other tourists, this is the place to go. Live music is scheduled most days of the week. A healthy beer selection of local, Pacific Northwest, and other regions has space on the taps. **167 S. Franklin St., Juneau | thealaskanhotel.com/alaskan-bar**

HANGAR ON THE WHARF: It's not just the bi-planes taking off and landing from the dock right out front that are impressive, it's also the 80+ beers in bottles and cans and the 24 taps. Domestic and local craft beers are plenty, as well as some imports, domestics, and ciders. The food menu is full of Alaskan seafood, steaks, sandwiches, and other specialties. Sit on the patio overlooking the wharf and treat yourself to some gorgeous views of mountains, water, cruise ships, and, of course, airplanes. Weekend evenings they host live music and other events. **2 Marine Wy., #106, Juneau | hangaronthewharf.com**

HAINES

HAINES BREWING CO.: An afternoon or evening in the beer garden is perfect for trying out the 9 fresh beers on tap, some of which include vintage ales that are served in snifter glasses. Our recommendations include Captain Cook's Spruce Tip Ale, Eldred Rock Red, and Black Fang. The tasting room has plenty of seating if an evening in is more to your liking. No food is prepared or served on site, so you'll want to bring your own snacks. **327 Main St., Haines | hainesbrewing.com**

HAWAII

What's better than catching some waves and some rays while drinking island-inspired beers? Not much. Hawaii has its share of breweries and beer bars that have been around for a while, with a crop of new ones emerging. The unique ingredients found fresh on the island state create some exciting opportunities for envelope-pushing brews.

BEST SPOTS FOR OLD SCHOOL BEER STYLES

Big Island Brewhaus brews Belgian and American craft-beers one batch at a time while Stewbum & Stonewall Brewing Co. whips up incredible beers true to traditional styles.

BEST SPOTS FOR NEW SCHOOL BEER STYLES

Beer Lab Hawaii creates experimental small batches of beer with interesting local ingredients (because it's Hawaii and coffee counts as a local ingredient, right?). Waikiki Brewing Company's Randall infusions add a creative twist to their core beers.

BEST SPOTS TO ENJOY A MEAL WITH YOUR BEER

REAL: A Gastropub offers beer-centric dishes served "tapas-style" and made from local and seasonal ingredients to accompany their extensive tap and bottle lists while Yard House Waikiki has everything for food- and beer-lovers alike.

MOST STYLISH TAPROOMS AND BARS

Square Barrels's bright modern craftsman interior is as inviting as it is pretty, and BREW'd Craft Pub is full of beautiful inlaid wood designs plus one wall features a mural showing the history of beer.

MOST AWARD-WINNING BREWERIES

Maui Brewing's 7 GABF and 6 WBC medals give it bragging rights on the islands, but Kona Brewing's 7 GABF medals aren't far behind. Big Island Brewhaus has come on strong more recently with GABF and WBC medals in 2014.

BEST UNIQUE BEER EXPERIENCE

At Home of the Brave Brewseum, you can sip a beer by the huge stone fireplace while viewing the largest private collection of World War II memorabilia.

MAUI

MAUI BREWING CO. BREWERY: Kick back for some board games and conversation at the tasting room, which has breathtaking views of Haleakala and Molokini. Reserve a tour time for $15, which includes the tour, tasting, a free beer, and a glass. Then check out one of their four flagship beers or a limited-release beer. We like the Coconut Hiwa Porter, Big Swell IPA, and the Bikini Blonde Lager! Thirty-two taps that serve up their own beer as well as beer from other breweries are in the tasting room, and you can also order cider, kombucha, and lemonade. Food trucks visit often, and it's also kid-friendly (but no dogs). **605 Lipoa Pkwy., Kihei | mauibrewingco.com**

MAUI BREWING CO. BREWPUB: A satellite brewpub to Maui Brewing, it also has an onsite brewery, 19 of their beers on tap, and a full-service kitchen. The chefs have incorporated the beers into many recipes, including the Hot Wings, BBQ sauce, Kalua Pork sliders, and the Pub Plate. Beer can be purchased to go in growlers and cans. **Kahana Gateway Center, 4405 Honoapiilani Hwy., #217, Lahaina | mauibrewingco.com/visit-our-brewpub/lahaina**

KOHOLA BREWERY: It's one of Hawaii's newest craft breweries, but it already has 10 beers under its belt. Our recommendations include the 88 Light RyePA, which is a lighter incarnation of their imperial rye IPA; Mean Bean, a coffee stout; and Pineapple Lokahi, a Pilsner brewed with some local pineapple. While there's no kitchen on site, frequent food trucks swing by the brewery so people don't go hungry. Dogs and kids are most definitely welcome. **910 Honoapiilani Hwy., Lahaina | koholabrewery.com**

THE BIG ISLAND

KONA BREWING CO.: We fell in love with their Longboard Island Lager, which scored a 93 in our blind-tasting panel and has also garnered a silver medal at the Great American Beer Festival. You might also try out the Big Wave Golden Ale, Castaway IPA, and Koko Brown. Brewery tours happen daily. Pizzas are a mainstay on the food menu, as well as local seafood. **75-5629 Kuakini Hwy., Kailua-Kona | konabrewingco.com**

HUMPY'S BIG ISLAND ALEHOUSE: This is a beer-lover's paradise, with 36 craft-beers on tap. Many are from local brewers, but there are domestic and European beers on their list as well. Much of the food menu includes seafood specialties, as well as barbecue, pizzas, and burgers. **5815 Alii Dr., Kailua-Kona | humpyskona.com**

HAWAII NUI BREWING COMPANY: Four beers made in small batches round out the list at Hawaii Nui: Kaua'i Golden Ale, Sunset Amber Ale, Hapa Brown Ale, and Southern Cross. The Hapa, an American brown ale with a bold, malty backbone balanced with some hops bitterness, won silver at the World Beer Cup. You might try the Southern Cross, a Belgian-style double red ale with notes of caramel, toffee, and a subtle hint of jackfruit. **275 E. Kawili St., Hilo | hawaiinuibrewing.com**

BIG ISLAND BREWHAUS: Hawaii's highest altitude brewery sits at 2,764 feet above sea level and serves up award-winning beers and local handcrafted food. Golden Sabbath, a Belgian strong with a big fruity character from its special Belgian yeast, won a bronze at the Great American Beer Festival.

White Mountain Porter is flavored with toasted coconut and a Hawaiian-grown coffee, and it won silver at the U.S. Open, and the same organization named the brewery one of the Top Ten Breweries in America for two years in a row. About 14 beers can be found at the brewery on tap, as well as a few guest taps and mixed drinks. They have an open mic night, live music some nights, too! **64-1066 Mamalahoa Hwy., Waimea | bigislandbrewhaus.com**

TROPICS ALE HOUSE: With 24 rotating taps of craft-beer, you'll never have the same experience twice. Many of the beers on tap come from local Hawaiian brewers, and there's a nice selection from all over the U.S. and Europe. Pizzas are crafted from dough that's made on site, but you'll also find pub fare, salads, and some meatier platters. Live music events occur frequently. **69-1022 Keana Pl., Waikoloa Village | tropicsalehouse.com**

OAHU

BEER LAB HAWAII: Not far from the University of Hawaii is this craft brewery and tasting room with 8 frequently rotating taps. The tasting room is spacious and laidback, with plenty of tables for seating. No food is served on site, so you can bring your own or order in. Some of the most sought-after brews include Saison d'Orange et Brett, The Truth, and Coffee Porter, and you might also try The Imposter (same beer as The Truth, but fermented with *Saccharomyces* instead of *Brett)* and The Mirage. Trivia nights are a mainstay here, as are Beer Brush Strokes where patrons can paint on canvas while enjoying a glass or two of beer. **1010 University Ave., Honolulu | beerlabhi.com**

HOME OF THE BRAVE BREWING & BREWSEUM: The brewery was started to honor America's Finest and those who have served in the U.S. military; it has a USO-style interior and boasts the largest private collection of World War II memorabilia in the Pacific. Notable brews include Pilot Pale Ale, Go for Broke Ale, and Remember Pearl Harbor Dark Lager. Their brew master is formerly of Odell's Brewing Company. Beers on tap include their own, as well as several other local breweries. Live music and trivia night are frequent events, and you can grab your beer to go in a growler. Food isn't served in the brewery itself, but in the brewseum next door, pizza and pretzels are on the menu, and sometimes an occasional food truck is on site. **Brewery: 909 Waimanu St., Honolulu | hotbbc.com / Brewseum: 901 Waimanu St., Honolulu | brewseums.com**

HONOLULU BEERWORKS: The brewery is a cool, comfortable place to hang out, with its recycled wooden walls, local art, two beer gardens, and outdoor seating. We recommend the Cocoweizen, which is a traditional Bavarian Hefeweizen with additions of toasted coconut, and the Hi-PA, a dank and resiny brew with notes of citrus fruits. Beer cocktails are also available. Food is on the menu, too, and features fresh local ingredients that play well with their onsite beers—salads, sandwiches, and snack foods, mostly. Yoga is sometimes available with advance ticketing. Growlers are available to go! **328 Cooke St., Honolulu | honolulubeerworks.com**

WAIKIKI BREWING COMPANY: There's a little bit of everything in the 8 beers on tap at Waikiki Brewing, from a light crisp blonde to a molasses porter, to a jalapeño amber. Look for the Eee Pah IPA, a 75-IBU brew made with three hops that has a great balance of bitterness and aroma. Or for something a little darker, try the Black Strap Molasses Porter, with bold choc-olate and coffee flavors, and of course black strap molasses. In addition to the 8 flagships, occasional special and limited-release beers might be on hand. Once a week, they create special Randall infusions that include fruit, dry hops, and other cool ingredients. Food is served on site, a mix of creative appetizer dishes, meaty entrees, and a few salads. Even though tours aren't available, the brewing operations can be seen right from the bar. Yoga and trivia nights are some of the events you might expect, but if relaxation is all that's on the menu, grab a seat in the outdoor beer garden. Growlers and kegs are available for purchase, and a can program is in its early stages. **1945 Kalakaua Ave., Honolulu | waikikibrewing.com**

REAL: For those who believe that variety is the spice of life, you'll want to make a stop here, where 34 beers are on a constantly rotating tap/cask, and well over 100 bottles are on hand. Beers come from all over Hawaii, the lower forty-eight, and Europe, so there's little chance you won't find something you like. And if something less beer-y is more your thing, take a look at the specialty beertail and cocktail menu. Upscale tapas dishes with really reasonable prices are made on site, made with local seasonal ingredients. **1020 Auahi St., Bldg. 1, Honolulu | realgastropub.com**

YARD HOUSE WAIKIKI: For more than 100 beers on tap that hail from Hawaii, the U.S., and all over the world, this is the place to go. Their Chalkboard Series features a rotating list of beers on tap that are selected monthly for being some of the most distinctive and complex beers from all over the world. The food menu is just as diverse as its beer list, with old favorites, new twists on favorites, and some dishes that are uniquely theirs. Yard House restaurants are located all over the U.S., and we thought this particular location was noteworthy because of its location, and the huge selection of beers and food—it's the perfect place to go when you're in a large group and nobody can agree on what to eat. **226 Lewers St., Honolulu | yardhouse.com/locations/hi/honolulu/waikiki-waikiki-beach-walk**

SQUARE BARRELS: Well-crafted beers and burgers are what you'll find at this downtown Honolulu restaurant. About 20 taps and 30 bottles are on hand, mostly selected from the finest breweries in Hawaii, Califor-nia, and Alaska, as well as a handful of other U.S. and international breweries. Mixed drinks are also on the menu. The dining room is bright and open, with lots of natural light from the floor-to-ceiling windows, and very family-friendly. The menu is divided into Burgers and Not Burgers, and the Not Burgers side has a nice mix of meat entries, salads, and pasta. **1001 Bishop St., Honolulu | squarebarrels.com**

TROPICS TAP HOUSE: Let's start with the beer. They've got just about ev-erything, from your cheap big box brew to some truly unique brews from all over the U.S. Fifty-four taps make up the draught offerings, and if that's not enough, ask for the bottle list. Beertails and cocktails are also on the menu! Now for the food. Much of it has beer as part of the recipe, and it's mostly beer-food apps, sliders, and pizzas. This is also a live music destination, so if you're up for some killer music with your beer and pizza, this is the place to be. **1019 University Ave., Honolulu | tropicstaphousehonolulu.com**

BREW'D CRAFT PUB: This is Real's sister location, a small pub setting and neighborhood craft-beer pub. About 20 beers are on tap, and the bottle list is anywhere from 100–200, featuring brews from all over the U.S. and the world. The food is tapas-style gastro fare that pairs well with the beers on hand, and uses beer in the recipes. **3441 Waialae Ave., Ste. A, Honolulu | brewdcraftpub.com**

TAMURA'S FINE WINE & LIQUORS: Four generations have overseen this market, which has swept up multiple local "best of" awards. A massive selection of craft-beers and seasonal and limited release beers can be found here, as well as liquor, wine, cigars, and specialty foods. And don't leave before you stop by the poke bowl bar, which is outstanding. **3496 Waialae Ave., Honolulu / 98-302 Kamehameha Hwy., Aiea / 25 Kaneohe Bay Dr., #106, Aikahi Park Shopping Center, Kailua | tamurasfinewine.com**

LANIKAI BREWING COMPANY: Its tasting room is tiny, they only serve tasters, and they brew in small batches, but don't let the size of their operations deter you. The three to four beers on tap are well-loved by the locals and include a few from their regular lineup and one special-release beer. The Pillbox Porter is made with Hawaiian and Tahitian vanilla beans, and is one not to miss when it's on tap. The Forever Summer P.O.G. Berliner Weisse is brewed with locally harvested passion fruit, mandarin oranges, and guava. Growler fills are available to go. **175-C Hamakua Dr., Kailua | lanikaibrewing.com**

STEWBUM & STONEWALL BREWING CO.: Although it's a small operation, it brews up some fantastic beers and is a destination for locals and tourists alike to visit. Kickstarter got this brewery up and running, and it's family owned and rich in history (each of its beers has a story, which the brewmaster is happy to share when you visit). Anywhere from three to four beers are on tap at a time. We highly recommend the Swear Jar American IPA and the Smoking Cannon Smoked Imperial Stout. Food can be brought in from one of the nearby restaurants, and growlers can be filled depending on availability. **46-174 Kahuhipa St., Kaneohe | stewbumandstonewall.com**

KAUAI

NANI MOON MEADERY: If you've got a hankering for mead, this is Hawaii's only meadery and clearly the place to be. The location allows for a rare selection of honeys, and fresh, local fruits found nowhere else. Some meads to try include the Cacao Moon, made with macadamia nut blossom honey and Kaua'i cacao and vanilla beans; Ginger Spice, made with island honey, starfruit, and organic ginger and winter spices; and Winter Sun, made with Kaua'i windflower honey, starfruit, and passionfruit. The tasting room serves up some really incredible cocktails made from the mead, and many of the recipes can be found on the website and Facebook page for those following along at home. Enjoy a flight of tasters on site, and grab a bottle to go—if you're not local, they're happy to ship them to you! **4-939 Kuhio Hwy., Kapaa | nanimoonmead.com**

KAUAI BEER COMPANY: This is your neighborhood microbrewery, providing a chilled-out ambiance and small artisan batches of brew. The beers are on a rotating tap, and one keg is on nitro. Our recommendations are Tropical Armadillo, IPAloha, and Bock Bock. Lunch and dinner (soups, salads, sandwiches, and pasta dishes) are served on site and use local farm-fresh ingredients. Sometimes food trucks stop by after lunch to serve up dinner instead of the regular dinner menu. **4265 Rice St., Lihue | kauaibeer.com**

INDEX

COLORADO

INDEX

INDEX

NOTES